# 101 Chillies

## to Try Before You Die

# 101 Chillies
## to Try Before You Die
### David Floyd

# Chilli heat levels

There are no official classifications for the heat levels in chillies, which are measured by Scoville Units (SHU) but these are the categories I use and the way that this book has been organized.

0 SHU Sweet

0–2,500 SHU Mild

2,500–100,000 SHU Warm

100,000–500,000 SHU Hot

500,000–1,000,000 SHU Very Hot

1,000,000+ SHU Super Hot

An Hachette UK Company
www.hachette.co.uk

First published in Great Britain in 2016 by
Cassell Illustrated, a division of
Octopus Publishing Group Ltd
Carmelite House
50 Victoria Embankment
London EC4Y 0DZ
www.octopusbooks.co.uk

ISBN 978-1-84403-844-2

A CIP catalogue record for this book is available from the British Library.

Printed and bound in China

10 9 8 7 6 5 4 3 2 1

Senior Commissioning Editor
  Eleanor Maxfield
Editor Pauline Bache
Copyeditor Jane Birch
Designers Jeremy Tilston and Jaz Bahra
Picture Research Manager
  Giulia Hetherington
Picture Library Manager Jen Veall
Assistant Production Manager
  Caroline Alberti

# Contents

# Introduction

Welcome to the world of fire and spice. Chillies and peppers are one of the fastest-growing areas in food with new brands and products launched all the time. Luckily, we can almost all grow chillies at home even if we have only a windowsill and a few small pots.

This book tries to cover as wide a range of chillies as possible, I have not just selected the hottest 101 chillies I could find as, while being very macho, they would also be very boring. So we start with some mild peppers and work our way up via interesting variations to the latest super hot chillies.

I hope along the way to show you to some new tastes and chilli styles that impressed me over the last 20 years working with chillies. I was first introduced to chillies in a big way when my career took me on frequent trips to California, where it was deemed fun to try to kill the Brit with the hottest Thai and Mexican food as they could find. Each time I returned home I would bring new sauces, dried chillies and recipes back to try on my friends.

During the years I have manufactured BBQ Rubs, had my own brand of chilli-flavoured crisps and chilli flavourings, sold chilli ice cream, written books and articles, and run a successful online chilli store and probably the world's largest chilli blog (www.chilefoundry.co.uk).

I hope you enjoy this book as much as I did researching it over the past 20-plus years.

## The common chilli species

There are currently just five commonly grown chilli species that we describe as cultivated, but there are many more wild species and maybe a few yet to be discovered. The common species are:

***Capsicum annuum*** This is the most popular of the cultivated species; the name comes from the mistaken idea that these are annuals and have to be grown each year. Examples include: Aleppo Pepper (see page 84), NuMex Heritage Big Jim (see page 86), Pepperdew™ Piquanté Pepper (see page 38), Jalapeño (see page 60), Poblano (Ancho) and Mulato (see page 34).

***Capsicum chinense*** Named by Dutch botanist Nikolaus Joseph von Jacquin in 1776, who believed they originated from China. Examples include: Carolina Reaper (see page 220), Orange Habanero (see page 178),

Scotch Bonnet (see page 180), Bhut Jolokia (see page 200).

***Capsicum baccatum*** The name 'baccatum' comes from the word 'baccate' which means berry-like, probably one of the first domesticated species of chillies with evidence dating it back to the Incas. Examples include: Ají Amarillo (see page 116), Criolla Sella (see page 98).

***Capsicum frutescens*** Often combined with *C. annuum*, but research by Paul G. Smith and Charles B. Heiser Jr. in 1957 identified this as a separate species, although it can take an expert to tell them apart. Examples include: Prik Kee Nu (see page 168), Tabasco (see page 126), Siling Labuyo (see page 158).

***Capsicum pubescens*** The name 'pubescens' refers to the small hairs found on the underside of the leaves and stalks, so pubescens means 'hairy'. Uniquely, if you cut a pod open, you will find the seeds of this species are black or very dark brown in colour. They will also not cross-breed with the other cultivated species. The flowers are a blue/violet colour. Examples include: Manzano (see page 94).

## Wild chillies

There are currently 26 species that are described as wild chillies. There is little published research on these and I am sure there will be some duplication as well as some new ones to be found.

Known wild chilli species include: *Capsicum buforum*, *C. cattingae*, *C. campylopodium*, *C. cardenasii/ulupica*, *C. chacoense*, *C. cornutum*, *C. dimorphum*, *C. dusenii*, *C. exile*, *C. eximium*, *C. galapaqoense*, *C. geninifolium*, *C. hookerianum*, *C. lanceolatum*, *C. leptopdum*, *C. longidentatum*, *C. minutiflorum*, *C. mirabile*, *C. parvifolium*, *C. praetermissum*, *C. rhomboideum*, *C. scottianum*, C. *scolnikianum*, *C. tovarii* and *C. villosum*.

Each of these species comes from different regions of South America, with the exception of the *C. galapaqoense*, which comes from the Galapagos Islands. There is a growing interest in wild chillies and you can often find seed at specialist websites, including www.fataliiseeds.net and www.tradewindsfruit.com

## Some key terms

**Open-pollination** is the natural process by which insects, etc. pollinate the plants. If you are growing a single variety without other varieties nearby, you are more than likely to get seeds that are descended from parents of the same strain of the species, but it is not guaranteed.

**Closed/controlled pollination** is what commercial seed producers do to make sure the seeds they produce stay true to the breed. To make sure there is no cross-pollination, they keep the plants isolated while the flowers form. Once the flowers drop and the pods start to grow, the seeds should be safely uncrossed. This does mean that the producers may have to pollinate the plants manually using a soft brush or cotton bud to move the pollen from the male to female parts of the flowers. Cross-pollination will have no effect on the pods you produce from a plant; it will affect only the seeds and therefore subsequent generations.

**De-hybridization** If you want to create your own open-pollinated variety from an F1 hybrid (see opposite) it is possible, but the process can be very time-consuming and good results are not guaranteed. To de-hybridize a plant you will need to collect seeds from many generations, each time carefully selecting only the plants with the characteristics you desire.

Some commercial crops are developed to have characteristics that are desirable to commercial growers, like having all the pods ripen at a similar time to help with harvesting. However the domestic grower may prefer to have a long sustained harvest so they can use the chillies over the season as they ripen.

The Super Chile is an F1 hybrid that has been very successful with the domestic grower, but over the last few years an open-pollinated variety called Super Tramp has been developed (see page 134). It shares many of the good characteristics of the Super Chile, like its tolerance to shade, quick maturity and high productivity, making it ideal for the home grower.

**Heirloom and heritage varieties** You will see some chillies described as heirloom and heritage varieties. There is not a strict definition of what makes a plant an heirloom or heritage variety but it does indicate that the plant is an open-pollinated variety, which is maintained over time by growers who appreciate its unique properties. Seeds of heirloom and heritage chillies have been carefully passed down through generations of growers. The history of these varieties is hard to trace to a single point, but they mostly come from ethnic groups or communities. Heirloom plants generally survive as they have become well suited to the conditions in a region or they show a particular variation that is valued by the grower. Now these varieties are being sought after, as most lack the uniformity and blandness that modern cross-breeding has created.

**Hangjiao** Translating to 'space pepper', these are seeds associated with the Chinese space rocket, Shijian-8, launched in 2006 with around 2,000 seeds, including peppers and chillies, some of which showed improvements in size, taste or nutritional value on their return. There seems to be no definitive explanation why a short trip to space alters these seeds, but they were exposed to cosmic radiation, zero gravity and changing magnetic fields.

**F1 hybrid** An F1 hybrid is created whenever you cross any two stable chilli varieties, the resulting plant being called an F1. Seeds from this plant would create an F2 hybrid. F2 hybrids are more unstable and this is why most of the time seed-saving from an F1 hybrid is not recommended.

**The Slow Food Foundation Ark of Taste** This is a database of small-scale produce, including chillies and peppers, that are under threat of being lost in an increasingly homogenized world. You can search the Ark of Taste at www.fondazioneslowfood.com/en/ark-of-taste-slow-food/ and have a look at what needs saving near you.

**Seed saver groups** There are a number of groups opening up in forums and on social media. On a more professional level there is also the Seed Savers Exchange (www.seedsavers.org), a non-profit organization that shares seeds from a massive range of plants, including chillies. Note that, when using their site, you will need to look under peppers as they have classified sweet peppers and chillies together. The exchange is based in the USA and there is a $100 minimum order for international sales, but you can club together with a few other chilli fans. The selection of seeds is amazing and it is one of the few places where you can get the Hussli Tomato Pepper (see page 30) as well as many other rare species.

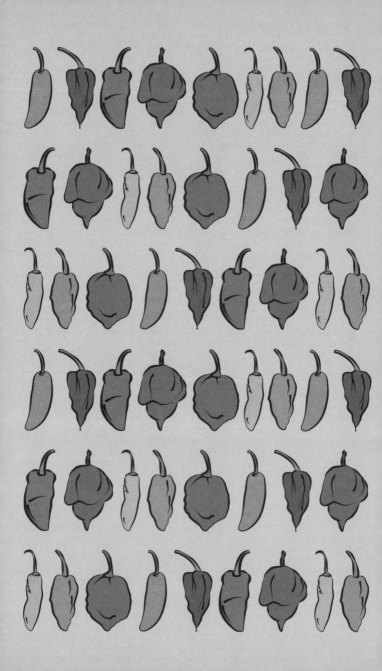

# Sweet & Mild

Jimmy Nardello

Tomato Pepper

Spike & Joker

Zavory Pepper

Cubanelle

Chilhuacle Negro

Apricot Habanero

Beaver Dam Pepper

Pimenta Bico

Hussli Tomato Pepper

Anaheim

Poblano (Ancho) & Mulato

Paprika

Peppadew™ Piquanté Pepper

Pimientos de Padrón

Cascabel

Kashmiri Mirch

Cherry Bomb

Guajillo

Trifetti Purple

Bulgarian Carrot

Hungarian Hot Wax

Friar's Hat

# 1 Jimmy Nardello

SPECIES

*C. annuum*

POD DESCRIPTION

Pods are 15–20cm long and 2–4cm wide, turning from green to a bright, shiny red.

GROWING INFO

Very productive, well worth growing but will need a greenhouse or polytunnel in cool-temperate climates.

SEED SUPPLIERS

BCS, MWCH, PSEU, PZW, SLP, TWF

How wonderful would it be to have a pepper variety named after you and saved for future generations. That is what has happened to Jimmy Nardello, whose pepper seeds are being kept in climate-controlled conditions by the Seed Savers Exchange in Decorah, Iowa (see page 9).

Originally from the Basilicata region of Italy, these peppers were the favourites of Angela Nardello who, with her husband Giuseppe and young daughter Anna, set sail for the USA in 1887 from Naples. They eventually settled in Naugatuck, a small town in Connecticut.

Jimmy was the family's fourth child of eleven and shared Angela's love of gardening. He passed away in 1983, but not before donating some of his pepper seeds to the Seed Savers Exchange.

For such a short plant, at only 50–60cm high, they produce a good crop of long, thin-skinned pods

SCOVILLE RATING

0 SHU

# 2
# Tomato Pepper

SPECIES

*C. annuum*

SCOVILLE
RATING

0–50,000
SHU

Surprisingly, there are quite a few Tomato Pepper varieties. Their claim to fame is that they have more than a passing resemblance to a tomato. As you can see from the picture, they more than just resemble tomatoes – the quick way to tell the difference between the two is to look at the calyx and stem. Once cut open, the Tomato Pepper is much like any other chilli variety.

Records of this style of chilli date back to 1613 when respected apothecary and botanist Basilius Besler illustrated a cherry pepper that looked very tomato shaped.

Tomato Peppers split into two main shapes: there are small, round, tomato-shaped pods, like the Weaver's Mennonite, Bombita F1 and the Ciliegia Piccante (AKA Baccio de Satana or Satan's Kiss); and the larger Red Ruffled Pimiento and the Italian Topepo Rosso, both of which are sweet peppers, which look more like beef tomatoes.

The Red Ruffled Pimiento produces beautiful 6–10-cm wide pods with thick flesh that ripens to a deep scarlet colour, while the Topepo Rosso is one of the best-flavoured sweet peppers.

The oddly named Sheepnose Pimento has the look of an overstuffed tomato but has also been described as apple shaped. While strictly a sweet pepper, it has been included in the Slow Food Foundation Ark of Taste (see page 9).

## POD DESCRIPTION

**There are two main shapes: small, round, tomato-shaped pods and those that look more like beef tomatoes. Both styles will ripen to a red colour to help with the tomato illusion.**

## GROWING INFO

**Tomato peppers are easy to grow, but check the description on the seed supplier site as some are more hardy than others.**

## SEED SUPPLIERS

**HS, LS, NN**

# 3

# Spike & Joker

**SPECIES**

*C. annuum*

**POD DESCRIPTION**

The upright, thin, spiky pods ripen from green to red, growing to 2–4cm long while just a few millimetres wide.

**GROWING INFO**

If you have one of these varieties, I think you must also grow the other. If you keep them in a small pot you will keep the plant small and manageable but it can take a while for the plant to mature and start producing.

**SEED SUPPLIER**

SSS

SCOVILLE UNITS

0–100,000 SHU

Spike and Joker are two separate varieties that have been developed from the same cross.

Spike is a low, bushy variety that produces thousands of very thin, elongated, pointed miniature pods that stick upwards from the plant, hence the name. Spike is best described as a vigorous grower and it will grow to fill any space you give it. A larger pot means a larger plant. The pods are very hot, measuring up to 100,000 SHU. Thus, this variety is ideal for the home gardener/cook and it is superb as a house plant in a small pot and very impressive in a larger space in a greenhouse.

Joker is identical in appearance to Spike in every way – grown side by side, it is impossible to tell them apart. However, Joker has NO heat whatsoever; although it looks like a chilli, it is heat-less. This means that Joker is NOT a chilli at all and, although it is very tempting to call it a very mild chilli, it is technically a sweet pepper.

As I understand it, Joker and Spike are genetically identical except for one gene, the gene that turns on the production of capsaicin. Joker, without the gene, is a sweet pepper, while Spike, with the gene, is a hot chilli.

# 4

# Zavory Pepper

SPECIES
............................
*C. chinense*

POD DESCRIPTION
............................
**Bright red pods grow
a little larger than the
typical Habanero at
about 3–4cm wide and
5cm long.**

GROWING INFO
............................
**Like most Habaneros,
it can take a while to
germinate and needs
a long, warm summer
to ripen. It is slow
to ripen, and is best
grown in a greenhouse
or polytunnel in cool-
temperate climates.**

SEED SUPPLIERS
............................
**BPC, CCN, SLP**

SCOVILLE
RATING
............................
10–100
SHU

Although a lot of time and effort have gone
into creating the super hot chillies, there are,
perhaps surprisingly and often overlooked in
our fascination with finding the hottest, other
growers who are expending the same time and
effort to make chillies milder, while trying to
retain the flavour of the hot variety. Zavory is one
such chilli.

This mild, very Habanero-style chilli was
developed by Dr Paul Grun at Pennsylvania State
University in the USA.

The Zavory really does look like a fiery
Habanero, making it ideal for a few tricks to be
played on the unsuspecting. The plant grows to
60–70cm high and can produce a good crop of
bright red pods.

There are other heatless Habanero-style
chillies and the Ají Dulce from Venezuela is
a popular variety, getting its name from the
Spanish for sweet, 'dulce' ('aji' being 'chilli'). It is
grown commercially in Venezuela and is used in
the local version of the tamale called the hallaca.

You may think, why not just use a sweet bell
pepper? Why waste your time on these? But these
chillies offer the flavours that make the Habanero
so popular and open a market for people who are
less heat-tolerant to enjoy them.

When I talk to even the most hardened hot-
heads, they always mention the flavour that the
extreme chillies provide as being the reason they
eat them. Myself, as I get older, find the heat kills
the flavour more quickly.

# 5 Cubanelle

SPECIES

*C. annuum*

SCOVILLE
RATING

200–1,000
SHU

This chilli is used in both Cuban and Puerto Rican cooking and in Italian cuisine. It is about as close as we get to a sweet bell pepper in this guide, but it is so much more.

The flavour is what you would hope of a good bell pepper, enhanced by the thinner flesh and mild heat. Cubanelles are truly excellent thinly sliced and added to a salad. The pods are mostly picked when still green, but they will get slightly hotter if left until they are fully mature and red.

The skin can be removed by roasting over an open flame and then carefully peeling with your fingers or the edge of a spoon. Do not wash the pods as they will lose their smoky flavour. They can then be stored in olive oil. In Italy they are known as the Frying Pepper and are simply split open, deseeded and lightly fried in olive oil.

This is one chilli pepper that I would welcome seeing replacing the bell pepper on our supermarket shelves.

### POD DESCRIPTION

**The pods start green and mature through to red. They grow to 10cm long and 4–5cm wide, tapering to a blunt tip.**

### GROWING INFO

**Don't grow bell peppers, grow this instead. Easy to grow, it is a low-maintenance plant that likes full sun.**

### SEED SUPPLIERS

**LS, SLP, PJ**

### AKA

**Ají Cubanela, Cubanella, Friarelli, Italian Frying Pepper, Pimiento de Cocinar.**

### USAGE

**Slice and add to salads, or roast and store covered in olive oil.**

# 6

# Chilhuacle Negro

SPECIES
........................
*C. annuum*

POD DESCRIPTION
........................
The large pods start
green and ripen to a dark
brown – almost black.
They are similar in shape
to a bell pepper, if a little
smaller at 7–10cm long
and 3–5cm wide.

GROWING INFO
........................
This is a large plant
which will need some
space. To fully ripen,
it will need warm
conditions and in cold
climates this will need
to be in a polytunnel to
reach its full potential.

SEED SUPPLIERS
........................
CCN, LS, NN, SLP

AKA
........................
Chile Negro, Mexican
Negro, Pasilla Bajio.

Like most big chillies, this is not going to set
the world alight in heat, but the flavour carries
more than just hints of warm chocolate with the
sweet scent of a rich pipe tobacco and dark dried
Christmas fruits.

Originally from the Mexican Oaxaca region,
where it likes the warm and mild climate,
Chiluacle Negro is used locally to make the
Oaxaca version of the Mexican national dish,
Mole Negro.

The Chilhuacle is listed in the Slow Food
Foundation Ark of Taste (see page 9) as the high
cost of growing it has meant a steady decline in
its production. Seeds are available, though not
common, but are well worth searching out.

Two other Chilhuacle chillies come from the
same area of Mexico. The yellow variety is known
as the Chilhuacle Amarillo and the Chilhuacle
Rojo is red. Again, although not commonly
available, these are well worth growing if you can,
although they differ in flavour from the Negro.

SCOVILLE
RATING
........................
250–1,500
SHU

# 7

# Apricot Habanero

**SPECIES**

*C. chinense*

**POD DESCRIPTION**

Slightly grooved pods, 2–3cm wide and up to 6cm long, that ripen from lime-green to salmon colour.

**GROWING INFO**

Compact and easy to grow in pots or grow-bags, it will need some support as the pods mature.

**SEED SUPPLIERS**

SSS

**USAGE**

Use it to introduce a new generation to the flavours without the tears.

Typically, the Habanero is something that the chilli novice will avoid, since, while the flavour is great, the after-effect of the heat takes some practice before it can be appreciated. There have been a number of mild or tamed chillies in the past, but often they lack more than just the heat – they seem to miss out on some of the flavours too.

Happily, the Apricot Habanero has all the flavour and, especially, the aroma. In fact, it is a particularly fragrant variety – break open a single pod and everyone will know it. The heat level is extremely mild at only around 700 SHU; it is so mild that young children have eaten it without knowing it was a chilli.

The plant is a prolific producer of beautifully even-shaped pods that ripen from lime-green to a lovely salmon colour. A great introduction to chillies, it can be grown in pots, grow-bags or even directly in the ground.

Slice a few of these and add them to a strong Cheddar cheese sandwich, or use them to make mild versions of any classic Mexican and Caribbean dishes.

**SCOVILLE RATING**

500–700 SHU

# 8 Beaver Dam Pepper

Originally from Hungary and brought to the Beaver Dam, Wisconsin, USA, area around 1912 by Joe Hussli who was also responsible for the Hussli Tomato Pepper (see page 30) from the same area.

This pepper was almost lost until it was added to the Slow Food Foundation Ark of Taste list in 2007 (see page 9).

Since October 2014 there has been a Beaver Dam Pepper Festival to celebrate this pepper.

SCOVILLE
RATING

500–1,000
SHU

# 9

# Pimenta Bico

SPECIES
............................

*C. chinense*

SCOVILLE
RATING
............................

**500–1,000
SHU**

From the Brazilian state of Minas Gerais comes the Pimenta Bico, AKA Chupetinha or Biquinho Pepper, which means 'pepper beak' or 'pepper dummy'. The plant grows to about 50cm high and produces an abundance of small, red or yellow pods (dependent on the variety).

I have come across recipes for pickling these pods in vinegar and salt. Unexpectedly, the recipes blanched the pods in boiling water before rapidly cooling in iced water. This would have the effect of making the skin more porous, but also of cleaning the pods so they would be less likely to spoil when pickled.

POD DESCRIPTION

Red or yellow pods that are 2–3cm in diameter. The pods are round with an elongated cone-shaped beak or nipple on the base, making some of them almost teardrop shaped.

GROWING INFO

Compact plant with small pods, but likes warm conditions. Set your propagator to 22°C.

SEED SUPPLIERS

PBPC, SLP, SSS, TWF

AKA

Biquinho, Chupetinha

# 10 Hussli Tomato Pepper

**SPECIES**

*C. annuum*

**POD DESCRIPTION**

The pepper grows to approximately 8cm in diameter, features very thick flesh and ripens from green to orange and then to a deep red.

**GROWING INFO**

If you can find seed, then grow them. If you like them, then pass some on to your mates. While these are open-pollinated (see page 8), this does not always happen because of cross-pollination with other nearby chillies. Seed producers work hard to keep plants from cross-pollinating.

**SEED SUPPLIERS**

None

This chilli is a small, heavy pepper which gets its name from its visual resemblance to a traditional-style tomato.

It is believed to have been brought to the USA by Joe Hussli who was also responsible for bringing the Beaver Dam Pepper (see page 26) to the same area around 1912.

Joe's family would sell this unique pepper only in its unripe green state so that the seeds would not be viable, thus making sure they had no competition. The latest grower in the family, Larry, has been growing them for over 45 years, giving away most of what he grows. He has also shared the seeds with other interested growers, making sure this variety is not lost.

The Slow Food Foundation has selected this pepper for its Ark of Taste (see page 9), so publicizing this pepper to a new group of people interested in food for the quality of the flavour, not just the ease of growth or the shelf life.

Hopefully, seeds for these will become available in seed catalogues and via online resellers, but at the moment you will have to search about a bit to find some and the best places would be the seed saver groups (see page 9).

SCOVILLE RATING

500–2,000 SHU

# 11 Anaheim

*C. annuum*

SCOVILLE
RATING

approx. 500–2,500
SHU

The Anaheim gets its name from the city of Anaheim, California, which today is probably better known for the number of theme parks than for the local agriculture. But in 1894, well before theme parks, Emilio C. Ortega introduced a chilli to the area that grew so successfully that it became known as the Anaheim Pepper. Emilio preserved the peppers by fire-roasting them to remove the skins; the peppers were then deseeded and finally washed before canning. His business, Ortega, is still producing canned Anaheim chillies to this day, as well as many other products.

They mature from green to red, but are most often used when still green. All the canned and bottled chillies produced by Ortega are in the green stage of maturity.

The pods have a thick, waxy, waterproof skin that should be removed before use. Traditionally, the method is to roast them over an open fire (a barbecue is good for this) until the skins are burnt and blistered, then seal them in a bag to let the heat further loosen the skin. When cooled, gently pull the burnt skin away from the flesh. If you want to have a little bit of a smoked flavour, do not wash off any remaining burnt flecks of the skin. They are now ready to be used or to be preserved.

They are a great chilli to stuff and can be used as an alternative to the Poblano chilli (see page 34) to make the dish Chilli Relleno (Spanish for 'stuffed chilli') in which the chilli is stuffed with cheese and then coated in an egg batter and deep-fried.

## POD DESCRIPTION

The Anaheim chilli grows up to 25cm long and up to 5cm wide. It matures from green to red.

## GROWING INFO

It can grow to almost 1m high and is big and bushy. It likes to be kept moist if it is to produce some nice big pods.

## SEED SUPPLIERS

HS, LS, NN, PZW, SDCF, SLP, SS

## AKA

California Chile, Magdalena and, when fully matured and dried, Chile Seco del Norte.

## USAGE

Excellent for stuffing.

# 12 Poblano (Ancho) & Mulato

SPECIES

*C. annuum*

SCOVILLE RATING

500–3,000
SHU

The Poblano is a very mild chilli from the Mexican state of Puebla, 'poblano' meaning 'pepper from Puebla'. The Poblano pods are heart shaped and can grow up to 8 × 15cm; they have thick flesh and ripen from a dark green to a chocolate-brown colour.

When dried, the Poblano changes its name to become the Ancho. When dried it is available all year and can be found in most specialist retailers. I sometimes use it shredded up and then lightly dry-fried and added to my ever-evolving chilli con carne recipe.

Now comes the confusion... the Mulato and Poblano are basically the same; they are just different varieties of Poblano which produce darker or lighter pods. What they are categorized as comes down to when the pods are sorted. The dark brown, almost black, pods are graded as Mulato while, if they are dark brown with a hint of red, they are called Poblano/Ancho. The difference in pod colour can depend how long they are left to ripen.

Note: To further add to any confusion, in some parts of southern California they call the Poblano a Pasilla, which elsewhere is a completely different variety.

## POD DESCRIPTION

**Mulato have dark brown pods while the Poblano/Ancho are lighter with a hint of red. They can grow to 7–15cm long and 5–7.5cm wide.**

## GROWING INFO

**Best grown in the ground, these plants will need support, otherwise they will often break under the weight of the ripening pods. The plants grow tall, easily reaching 1m high, and will need plenty of space.**

## SEED SUPPLIERS

**BPC, BS, CB, CCN, CH, CSB, MWCH, NMSU, NN, PJ, PSEU, PZW, RMR, SDCF, SLP, SS, SSS, TCPC, TF, TWF, UKCS, VNG**

## AKA

**Pasilla (in southern California).**

# 13 Paprika

SPECIES
..........................................
*C. annuum*

SCOVILLE
RATING
..........................................
500–10,000
SHU

Paprika is not a single chilli pepper variety, but comes from a number of pepper varieties, all known for their strong red colour.

When many people think of Paprika, they think of Hungary, but Paprika is also grown in quantity in Spain, Serbia and Holland (in large greenhouses), as well as in the USA. While Hungary may be the home of Paprika, Spain produces its own versions, in particular Pimentón de la Vera, with its smoky aroma, which comes from being dried and smoked using oak, the whole process taking about two weeks.

Hungary takes Paprika very seriously. There is even a dedicated museum in the town of Szeged which, with nearby Kalocsa, is the heart of Hungarian production. The industry became mechanized in 1859 when the Pálfy brothers from Szeged opened a Paprika mill that removed the seeds and veins before grinding the pods.

In 1937, Hungarian scientist Dr Szent-Györgyi was awarded the Nobel Prize for isolating vitamin C in Paprika. He also discovered that Paprika, and therefore chillies, contains more vitamin C than oranges.

Lots of varieties can be made into Paprika, the common factor being the strength of the colour. Look out for known varieties such as Leutschauer Paprika Pepper, Alma Paprika and Dulce Rojo Paprika, which is a firm favourite, being mild and one of the easiest to grow.

### POD DESCRIPTION

**Each variety produces different-shaped pods but all mature to the deep red needed for a classic Paprika.**

### GROWING INFO

**Lots of variation with the varieties, but they like a well-drained, fertile and sunny position, and are very susceptible to frost.**

### SEED SUPPLIERS

**BCS, CH, LS, PBPC, PJ, PSEU, PZW, RFC, SLP, SS, TCPC, TWF**

### AKA

**Pimentón de la Vera**

### USAGE

**Traditionally, the pods would be air dried before grinding into powder.**

# 14

# Peppadew™ Piquanté Pepper

SPECIES
..................................

*C. annuum*

POD DESCRIPTION
..................................

The round pods grow to 3–4cm in diameter. They start green and mature via bright orange to red with a glossy skin and thick juicy flesh.

GROWING INFO
..................................

Successfully farmed on a massive scale in South Africa, so should not be too hard to grow if you are able to find an official source of seeds.

SEED SUPPLIERS
..................................

HS (for Malawi Piquanté), RFC

USAGE
..................................

Pepperdew™ peppers available to buy have been processed, and have the seeds removed before being preserved in a sweet brine.

SCOVILLE RATING

900–1,100 SHU

The Pepperdew™ Piquanté Pepper is one of the few peppers for which you cannot officially buy seeds nor even grow your own plants. It was discovered growing in Port Elizabeth, South Africa, by farmer Johan Steenkamp in 1993. He cleverly recognized the potential of this pepper, collected the seeds and developed his find into a stable chilli that could be protected by PVP (Plant Variety Protection).

The PVP gives plant developers 25 years' protection. You cannot get it for any variety of chilli; only new, distinct, uniform and stable varieties (the Dorset Naga, see page 208, has also been through this rigorous process).

All the Pepperdew™ products are grown in the Limpopo and Mpumalanga provinces and the first products were introduced in 1996 in South Africa. Growing and processing are controlled by one company with strict growing contracts. While the PVP does not stop home growers saving seeds and growing their own, there has not yet been an official source of the seeds.

I have listed the Pepperdew™ as a *Capsicum annuum*. Many descriptions speculate that it is a *C. baccatum*, but it is listed as *C. annuum* in a 1998 copy of the Australian *Plant Varieties Journal* as part of the local PVP application.

There are varieties of chillies very similar to the Pepperdew™ that you could grow at home. The Malawi Piquanté, for example, looks very similar in size and shape, but is listed as a *C. baccatum*. I have also come across 'Pepperdew' seeds for sale on eBay and Amazon, which may be genuine.

# 15 Pimientos de Padrón

SPECIES

*C. annuum*

SCOVILLE RATING

1,000–5,000 SHU

This chilli is in the top 101, not for its extreme heat, of which it provides very little, but for the way it is eaten. The Pimientos de Padrón have become part of the Spanish tapas craze that has spread around the world.

The name comes from the municipality of Padrón in northwest Spain where they are grown. It is said that they were brought back from South America in the 16th century by missionaries. So famous have these chillies become that, since 1979, they have been celebrated by holding the Festa do Pemento de Padrón each August in Herbón near Padrón.

Preparation is simple. The peppers are fried in a heavy pan with a little olive oil until the skin just starts to char and blister. They are then sprinkled with a little sea salt and served. Eat them just by holding the stem and biting off the fleshy chilli.

They are best harvested when immature, when 2.5–4cm long. They should be bright to yellowish green with curved furrows along the skin. If left to mature they will grow to 10cm and turn a bright red. At this point they will all be hot, again not searing, but at just about 3,000 Scoville Units. So if you grow some and you are not getting any hot ones you will need to let them mature a little longer and try again.

POD DESCRIPTION

Pods begin bright green and mature to bright red. They grow to 10cm.

GROWING INFO

This is a fairly simple pepper to grow. It enjoys full sun, and seed germination needs 18°–22°C. The plant will grow to about 50cm high. With the right conditions it will produce pods from late spring to mid-autumn and even late autumn if you are lucky.

SEED SUPPLIERS

BCS, CB, CH, LS, NN, PSEU, RFC, SDCF, SLP, SSS, TCPC, TWF

USAGE

If you do forget a few and let them mature, they are great stuffed with cheese or chilli con carne and baked.

# 16   Cascabel

SPECIES

*C. annuum*

SCOVILLE
RATING

1,500–2,000
SHU

Cascabel is Spanish for 'rattle' – these chillies get their name because of the sound they produce after they have been dried and the loose seeds rattle about inside.

Grown commercially in Mexico, they tend to be most readily available in dried form. Make them into a purée by cutting them open and removing the seeds, then dry-frying in a pan. Add the dry-fried chillies to some just-off-the-boil water and allow to steep for 12–15 minutes before blending into a smooth paste. This purée is best used within a few days. Why not try spreading some on the skin of a chicken before roasting, or add to some olive oil and then drizzle over a salad or on to tomato soup?

## POD DESCRIPTION

**The fresh pods grow to about 3cm in diameter in the shape of a stubby plum tomato, starting green and maturing to red. When dried, they take on a rich, dark brown colour.**

## GROWING INFO

**Let these ripen to fully red before harvesting and then dry for the best flavour and colour. Seeds from dried supermarket pods may not germinate as they have been frozen and processed.**

## SEED SUPPLIERS

**SLP**

## AKA

**Chilli Bola (Spanish for 'ball chilli'), Coras (when dried), Guajones (when dried), Jingle Bell, Rattle chilli.**

## USAGE

**A very useful chilli, which can be used fresh in salsa or stuffed with cream cheese. It is best to remove the seeds as they almost fill the skin. When dried, they make an excellent powder or chilli flakes, ideal for soups and casseroles.**

# 17 Kashmiri Mirch

SPECIES

*C. annuum*

SCOVILLE
RATING

1,500–2,000
SHU

The Kashmiri Mirch chilli is a mild chilli from India that is used to impart its deep red colour to Indian dishes such as Rogan Josh and is the Indian equivalent of Hungarian Paprika (see page 36). It is also found in the spice blend Deggi Mirch, which is made from chillies selected to give a consistent natural colour.

So popular is the Kashmiri chilli that demand has outstripped supply, with fake Kashmiri powder becoming common. I have never seen fruits sold fresh but always as dried chillies or as chilli powder. I like to buy them dried whole and grind them myself. You can also rehydrate them to make a paste by soaking them in warm water for ten minutes and then using a blender or a large pestle and mortar to make a paste, which can then be stirred into your curry dishes during cooking.

Kashmiri chilli seeds are available from some specialist suppliers, but I have grown them from seeds collected from the dried pods purchased in my local Indian supermarket. While germination rates have not been very high (you never know how old the pods are), you do get a lot of seeds this way. I have struggled to get mine to fully ripen.

## POD DESCRIPTION

The pods grow to 6–9cm long and 3–5cm wide with a gently curving body tapering to a point.

## GROWING INFO

Likes the warm conditions of a greenhouse or polytunnel in cool-temperate climates.

## SEED SUPPLIERS

PSEU, SLP, UKCS

# 18 Cherry Bomb

SPECIES

*C. annuum*

POD DESCRIPTION

The slightly pointed, round pods ripen from dark green to red and can grow to about 6cm long and 4cm wide.

GROWING INFO

Both the Cherry Bomb F1 and the Rodeo are easy to grow and very productive. They are early to produce pods; pick these as soon as they ripen to keep the plant productive. Plants like full sun and make ideal pot plants. They look nice and compact and will grow to about 60cm high.

SEED SUPPLIERS

BS, CH, LS, NN, PBPC, SS

I am not sure if the Cherry Bomb get its name from the small explosive device whose name it shares, but they can look very similar. The explosive device is a small ball of resin mixed with a filler, such as sawdust, with a core of some pyrotechnic mix and a short fuse sticking out the top. The chilli is a small, ball-shaped pod with a green stem sticking out the top.

Note that there is also a strain of marijuana called Cherry Bomb – you have been warned.

This is a prolific little chilli plant that has become very popular as it is so simple to grow and produces such a successful crop. The Cherry Bomb is an F1 hybrid (see page 9) from US specialist seed company Seminis. As an F1 variety, saving seeds will not produce the same chilli, but there is now a good open-pollination alternative called the Rodeo. It is one of the easiest chillies to grow and it is slightly more upright than the Cherry Bomb.

One of the best and simplest ways to process the pods is to cut them in half and remove the seeds; they can then be frozen for later use. If you carefully cut off the top and discard the seeds they make an excellent little chilli to stuff with a cheese mix and then bake or grill.

SCOVILLE
RATING

2,500–5,000
SHU

# 19 Guajillo

SPECIES

*C. annuum*

SCOVILLE
RATING

2,000–5,000
SHU

The Guajillo is the dried version of the Mirasol chilli with a tough, thick skin and thin flesh. Mirasol means 'looking at the sun', which becomes obvious when you see these chillies pointing through the leaves. With the pods growing erect, they are easy for manual harvesting.

After the Jalapeño (see page 60), this is one of the most popular chillies grown in Mexico. In some regions they are used as part of the Mexican national dish Mole, the dark red/brown colour of the dried pods complementing the colour of the dish.

The dried Guajillo make an excellent but simple thick sauce with the addition of just a few basic ingredients. First slit open 10–12 Guajillo pods and remove the seeds and stems, then dry-fry the skins for a couple of minutes before soaking them in a little hot water for 20–30 minutes (retain the water for later use). Place the chillies and a little of the water in a blender or food processor and reduce to a fine paste.

Add 2–3 cloves of fresh garlic and some oregano (Mexican is best here, if you are able to get hold of it). Add a little salt and continue to blend adding the reserved water as needed to make a fine paste.

Make a sauce to smear on chicken as a marinade before cooking, or as a sauce on tortillas. Swirl some into baked beans for the ultimate beans on toast.

Seeds are available, but it can be easier just to buy the pods dried as they are grown in such large numbers.

## POD DESCRIPTION

**Pods ripen to a dark red, and are about 10–14cm long and 3–5cm wide with a smooth skin and conical shape.**

## GROWING INFO

**Grows to about 60cm high, likes it moist but not wet, enjoys a warm, sunny position and to be well fed (sounds like me).**

## SEED SUPPLIERS

**CH, CSB, CSU, NMSU, SLP**

# 20 Trifetti Purple

SPECIES

*C. annuum*

POD DESCRIPTION

Small, stubby pods, up to 3cm long and 2cm wide, that mature from green to purple to red.

GROWING INFO

Being easy to germinate, this makes an ideal pot plant and can be grown inside or outside.

SEED SUPPLIERS

BPC, CB, CH, HS, LS, NN, PSEU, SLP, TCPC

AKA

Purple Tiger

This is a stunning-looking ornamental plant with variegated leaves of white, purple and green making it a very decorative pot plant.

It produces lots of pods, which start green, turn purple and then, finally, red. As the colour changes, the pods can take on two colours. Green pods get dark purple stripes, becoming lighter as the green colour fades and the red colour appears. The red combines with the purple to produce darker purple stripes that then fade to a bright red.

This is one of the simplest chillies to germinate and grow. It can be grown easily indoors or outside on a patio.

SCOVILLE RATING

2,000–6,000 SHU

# 21 Bulgarian Carrot

SPECIES

*C. annuum*

POD DESCRIPTION

The pods, which mature to a beautiful orange, grow up to 10cm long and about 2.5cm wide.

GROWING INFO

The plants grow to about 60cm and should produce a good crop of pods. They are a great early season variety. Like most chillies, they like full sun and can be grown in large pots on a sunny patio.

SEED SUPPLIERS

BPC, BS, CSB, HS, LS, NN, PZW, SDCF, SLP, SS, VNG

AKA

Shipkas

USAGE

Ideal chopped up in a salad or used to make jelly.

This heritage variety (see page 8) from Bulgaria/Hungary produces beautiful carrot-shaped pods that start green and mature through yellow until turning orange when fully mature.

You can really appreciate the colour when making delicious Bulgarian Carrot Jelly, perhaps adding raisins or sultanas.

SCOVILLE RATING

2,000–8,000
SHU

# 22 Hungarian Hot Wax

Hungarian Hot Wax is one of those standard
varieties that belongs in any top ten list, let alone
a top 101 list. It is a dependable variety, producing
a heavy crop of banana-shaped, fleshy pods that
ripen from a pale yellow to orange then red.

They are a low to medium heat with a good
flavour, making them a very useful and versatile
chilli in the kitchen. For people who do not crave
especially hot food, Hungarian Hot Wax can
satisfy all their chilli cooking needs, acting as
a vegetable and a spice chilli. This makes this
variety the chilli of choice for home gardeners
who will be only growing one or two chilli plants.

Do not be confused by the inclusion of 'Hot'
in the name; it does not mean the fruits are very
hot, just that they are chillies rather than sweet
peppers. The term 'Wax' is used to describe the
glossy sheen of the skin; most of the wax-type
peppers are sweet peppers, not chilli peppers.

SCOVILLE
RATING

2,000–8,000
SHU

# 23 Friar's Hat

SPECIES

*C. baccatum*

POD DESCRIPTION

The distinctive, winged pods start light lime-green and mature to a bright red. They can grow to around 6cm wide and long.

GROWING INFO

They like a warm 20°C outside temperature and in cool-temperate climates these do best in a greenhouse. They can seem to take an age to ripen.

SEED SUPPLIERS

BS, CSB, PBPC, SS

AKA

Ají Flor, Bishop's Crown, Bishop's Hat, Cambuci, Campane, Christmas Bell, Joker's Hat, Monk's Hat, Pimenta Cambuci, Tinkerbell, Ubatuba Cambuci.

USAGE

Their crispness makes them ideal in a fresh salsa or sprinkled over a salad.

This three- or four-sided chilli is most unusual in that it is wider than it is long. It is named Friar's or Bishop's Hat, after the hat often worn by bishops, the shape of which could be said to be similar. With its winged, almost flying-saucer look, it does make a good talking point.

The plant needs space to grow, reaching up to 2m high, but can produce a good crop of 50–100 pods and is good for overwintering.

There are a number of variations on the name of this chilli (see left). They may not all be the exact same variety, but I suspect they share a common heritage. A larger version of the Friar's Hat called the Nepalese Bell is also worth growing if you can find seeds.

SCOVILLE RATING

2,000–10,000 SHU

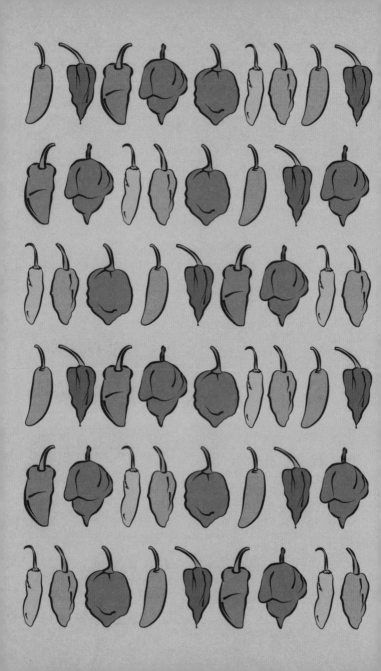

# Warm

Jalapeño

Sport Pepper

Espelette Pepper

Wenk's Yellow Hot Pepper

Chimayó

Urfa Biber

Pasilla de Oaxaca

Chipotle

NuMex Sunrise, Sunset & Eclipse

Ací Sivri Pepper

Fish Pepper

NuMex Mirasol

Aleppo Pepper

NuMex Heritage Big Jim

Serrano

De Arbol

Facing Heaven

Manzano

Cayenne Pepper

Criolla Sella

Black Pearl

Joe's Long Cayenne

Peter Pepper

Poinsettia

Shata Baladi

Yatsafusa

Demon Red

Diavolilli

Ají Amarillo

Bangalore Torpedo

NuMex Twilight

Pusa Jwala

Sibirischer Haus Paprika

Tabasco

Dundicut

Goat Horn Pepper

Bacio di Satana

Super Chile F1 & Super Tramp

Purple Haze

Cheiro Roxa

Coffee Bean

Tepin & Pequin

Ají Cereza

Murupi Amarela

Ají Pinguita de Mono

Apache F1

Turtle Claw & Submarine

Thai Dragon

Prairie Fire

Siling Labuyo

Wiri Wiri

# 24 Jalapeño

SPECIES

*C. annuum*

SCOVILLE
RATING

2,500–10,000
SHU

Taking its name from the capital of the Veracruz region of Mexico, Jalapa (or Xalapa), the Jalapeño is the world's most popular chilli and it seems to be everywhere. It has been included in apps and videogames (as in *Plants Vs Zombies* where exploding Jalapeño destroy a complete row of zombies) and Texas even designated the Jalapeño its state pepper in 1995.

Generally thought of as a mild variety, there have been efforts to make Jalapeño milder by cross-breeding with the bell pepper. Known as the TAM Mild Jalapeño or Tamed Jalapeño and developed by Dr Villalon at Texas A&M University, it rates at only around 1,000 SHU. This release in 1981 helped push revenue sales of salsa past those of ketchup in the USA and opened up a new market area for people who found even the Jalapeño too hot.

With its thick flesh, the Jalapeño is not easy to sun-dry, so at the end of the growing season they are left to ripen to red and then dried over the heat and smoke of large, well-controlled wood fires. The resulting dried and smoked chilli is known as the Chipotle (see page 74).

The Jalapeño includes many different varieties, each with their own special characteristics. One seed catalogue lists 28 varieties, each based on the original but bred to provide some specialist requirement. For instance, there are larger pods like the Huachinango, Jalapeño Jumbo and the Jalapeño Goliath F1, as well as varieties with higher heat levels and early cropping varieties like the Centella and Tamayo.

## POD DESCRIPTION

Generally bought in its green, immature state, it ripens to a dark crimson. The pods are often bullet shaped, with almost parallel sides and a rounded end. A particular characteristic (not found in supermarket versions) is 'corking' of small, brown lines on the skin, considered a much sought-after sign of quality in Mexico.

## GROWING INFO

Easy but requires lots of sunlight and frequent watering. Harvest often to keep producing, but don't forget we tend to eat them when they are still immature.

## SEED SUPPLIERS

BPC, BS, CCN, CH, CSB, CSU, HS, MWCH, NMSU, NN, PBPC, PJ, PN, PSEU, PZW, SDCF, SSS, TF, TWF, UKCS, VNG

## USAGE

Everywhere including on pizzas and nachos, as the flavouring for snacks, or stuffed with cream cheese as a Jalapeño Popper.

# 25

# Sport Pepper

SPECIES

*C. annuum*

POD DESCRIPTION

**These long slender pods will ripen to red, but are best used when green. They grow to 4–5cm long and 1.5cm wide.**

GROWING INFO

**Easy to grow and should produce a good crop. Pick the pods at the immature green stage.**

SEED SUPPLIERS

**MWCH, PSEU**

USAGE

**Pickled in vinegar.**

This probably isn't a real pepper variety, but if you visit Chicago you will find jars of these everywhere – they are a traditional topping for a Chicago-style hot dog. The pods are pickled in a white vinegar with just a little salt.

A Chicago hot dog is a work of art in its construction. Starting with a 100 per cent beef hot dog and a long, poppy-seed bun, the toppings include American yellow mustard, a green pepper relish, chopped sweet onions, tomato slices, a couple of pickled dill slices, at least two Sport Peppers and then a light sprinkling of celery salt.

I would say Sport Peppers were similar to Long Thai-style pods but having said that, it seems that I could be proved wrong, as a number of seed companies are selling seeds called Sport Pepper or Sport Chilli, which they describe as like a Tabasco (see page 126), but larger.

Making your own pickled Sport Peppers could not be simpler. Take 20–30 thin green Thai chillies or (Sport Peppers, if you can find them)). Wash them and then make a small hole in the top and near the bottom of each with a cocktail stick. Then add them to large stainless pot with 1 litre of white vinegar and a couple of teaspoons of salt and bring to the boil and simmer for 2–3 minutes. Carefully place the chillies lengthways in a sterilized jar and pour over the hot vinegar, seal the jar and let them cool. Once cooled they are best stored in the refrigerator and after a couple of weeks you will have, as near as possible, genuine Sport Peppers.

SCOVILLE
RATING

2,500–10,000
SHU

# 26 Espelette Pepper

SPECIES

*C. annuum*

POD DESCRIPTION

They can grow to 8–12 cm
long and 3–4 cm wide
with a slight curve to
thick, cylindrical, red
pods. When dried they
take on a darker red
colour.

GROWING INFO

This chilli has been
acclimatized to its native
environment and soil
conditions – a little
acidic and free draining
– over many years.

SEED SUPPLIERS

BPC, NMSU, SDCF,
SLP, SS

AKA

Ezpeletako Bipera,
Piment d'Espelette.

SCOVILLE
RATING

3,000–6,000
SHU

The Espelette Pepper comes from the northern
Basque area in France. All production takes
place between the ten villages of the Pyrénées-
Atlantiques (Ainhoa, Cambo-les-Bains,
Espelette, Halsou, Itxassou, Jatxou, Larressore,
Saint-Pée-sur-Nivelle, Souraïde and Ustaritz).

The story goes that the pepper was introduced
to the region in 1523 by a Basque navigator,
Gonzalo Percaztegi, who travelled with
Christopher Columbus on his second American
voyage. The Espelette is now protected by
AOC (Appellation d'Origine Contrôlée) status
at national level, and by PDO (Protected
Designation of Origin) certification at European
level. The AOC covers the chillies sold as powder,
on cords (like *ristras*, which are colourful strings
of dried chillies) and whole and fresh in small,
open boxes. Interestingly, the AOC does not cover
bulk or individual pods, plants or seeds. All of
the products must be produced, transformed
and packaged within geographical boundaries
specified by identified and authorized operators.

This prized pepper even has its own festival
which started in 1967. In 2017 they will be
holding the 50th festival, making it the oldest
chilli festival in the world.

You can get seeds for this pepper and grow
them at home, but, as is the case with the
Chimayó chilli (see page 68), a lot of what makes
this pepper special is what the French call
*terroir*. The unique Basque region, its climate
and growing conditions come together to make
something exceptional.

# 27 Wenk's Yellow Hot Pepper

**SPECIES**

*C. annuum*

**POD DESCRIPTION**

The pods grow to 5–10cm long and are similar to a Jalapeño (see page 60) in shape, but with a more waxy skin.

**GROWING INFO**

Seeds for this are rarer than might be expected for such a well-known variety. It is easy to grow and is a good producer. Pick the pods at all stages of development and keep Erris's heritage alive.

**SEED SUPPLIERS**

CCN, SLP, TCPC

There are some names that just seem to stand out and Erris Wenk, the developer of the Wenk's Yellow Hot Pepper, is one of those names. Little seems to be known about this farmer from Albuquerque, New Mexico, but his chilli lives on in seed collections.

This chilli was developed over many years to suit the growing conditions in Albuquerque. For a variety that is called Wenk's Yellow, it may seem strange that, while this chilli does start a pale yellow, to reach its full potential it will turn orange and then fully ripen to red.

You will find the Wenk's Yellow listed in the Ark of Taste (see page 9), so please grow and pass some of these on to further generations. Isn't it time we saw a Wenk's Pickle at a local food festival?

SCOVILLE
RATING

3,000–8,000
SHU

# 28 Chimayó

This is another regional speciality pepper which comes from the town of the same name Chimayó in New Mexico, USA. This one was another that was nearly lost or, at least, confused as other chillies were being passed off as Chimayó.

The history of this chilli possibly dates back to the 1500s when chillies were first introduced to the area by Spanish explorers.

Just a few years ago it was being grown by just three farmers. Now, thanks to the work of a non-profit group called The Chimayó Chile Farmers Inc., which was founded in 2005 to work with local farmers, this chilli is making a comeback.

In 2005, José Alfonso and Victoria Martinez donated Chimayó seeds to the project and, by 2007, the project had been able to provide 21 new growers with seeds.

In 2006, the group worked with local farmers to apply for a trademark for Chimayó to provide legal protection and, in 2009, they were granted a registered certification mark.

While you may be able to grow this chilli at home, part of what makes it special are the conditions in which it grows in New Mexico, similar to the *terroir* concept for grapes and wine. Here, the special characteristics – the geography, geology and climate of Chimayó – interact with the plant genetics.

**SCOVILLE RATING**

4,000–6,000 SHU

# 29 Urfa Biber

SPECIES
................................................

*C. annuum*

POD DESCRIPTION
................................................

The fresh pods are large,
at 7–10cm long.

This chilli comes from a region in Turkey called Şanlıurfa, where it is grown and processed. A simple explanation of the name is that in Turkish *Biber* means 'pepper' and 'Urfa' is the local shortened name for 'Şanlıurfa'.

This is one of the few processed chillies that is probably almost impossible to recreate at home. Although seeds are available so you can grow the plants yourself, the pods are uniquely processed. They are sun-dried during the day and then wrapped tightly at night to retain the moisture. The resulting pods are then crushed to produce the dark reddish-purple flakes that you would think had been rubbed in a light oil.

### GROWING INFO

Not hard to grow, but the uniqueness of this pepper is the way the pods are processed.

### SEED SUPPLIERS

BPC, MWCH, RFC, TCPC, UKCS

### USAGE

Try adding some flakes to roasted vegetables or when making a soup. The flakes are also good sprinkled on scrambled eggs and you can add the flakes to a bottle of olive oil and leave to infuse for home-made chilli oil. The fresh pods are ideal sliced and added to a salad.

SCOVILLE RATING

4,000–9,000 SHU

# Pasilla de Oaxaca

SPECIES

*C. annuum*

POD DESCRIPTION

**You will find these dried and sold in packs. These chillies are 10–14cm long and 4cm wide tapering to 2–3cm at the base.**

GROWING INFO

**Some seeds are available but there is a lot of confusion over what is the fresh variety that produces the Pasilla de Oaxaca; it may be that there is no single variety that is the true Pasilla de Oaxaca. Whichever variety you select to grow, remember that these expect a warm environment and plenty of sun.**

SEED SUPPLIERS

NMSU

SCOVILLE
RATING

4,000–10,000
SHU

This is a smoke-dried chilli from the Mixe region in the state of Oaxaca in Mexico. Oaxaca is famous for the range of chillies it produces, including the Chilhuacle Nego, Chilhuacle Roja and Chilhuacle Amarillo, but the rarest of them all is the Pasilla de Oazxaca.

There is some confusion as the Poblano and its dried forms, the Ancho and Mulato (see page 34), are often called Pasilla in southern California, while the more common Pasilla mentioned in recipes and found in specialist stores is a long, thin, dried Chilaca chilli.

It may be that the true fresh version of the Pasilla de Oaxaca is the Chilli de Agua, which translates as 'water chilli'. This 10–14-cm long and 2–3cm wide chilli is grown in small quantities and it is also rumoured that this was the chilli that was used to create the original Chilli Relleno (see page 33), which is now made almost exclusively with Poblano chillies.

Pasilla de Oaxaca is one of the chillies I would most like to try fresh. With so few being grown and even fewer smoked and dried, I have tried for years to get hold of some fresh pods. This chilli should probably be included in the Slow Food Foundation Ark of Taste (see page 9) before it completely disappears.

Smoked chillies have become a sensation in the past few years, with the Chipotle (see page 74) becoming the flavour of choice for adding to almost anything. Maybe the Pasilla de Ozaxaca could have such a future.

# 31    Chipotle

SPECIES
......................................

*C. annuum*

SCOVILLE
RATING
..................................
5,000–10,000
SHU

This is the chilli that we seem to being seeing added to almost everything, and it is not even a real chilli variety. The name Chipotle comes from the Nahuatl (Aztec) language and basically means 'smoked chilli pepper'.

The Chipotle is a smoked Jalapeño chilli (see page 60). The Jalapeño is normally eaten when green, but at the end of the growing season it is left to turn red and the mature Jalapeños are then smoked to preserve them.

There are two main types of Chipotle, the Meco and the Morita. The Morita is smaller than the Meco and is smoked for less time. It has a dark red exterior and is generally the cheaper of the two. The Meco, while larger, also has a smoked, dusty look to it and of the two has a much more smoky and robust flavour.

There is also the Chipotle Grande, which is a smoke-dried Huachinango chilli. This is a Jalapeño-type chilli but, at 10–15cm long, it is much larger.

To make things even more confusing, there is also the Jalapeño Chico, which is a Jalapeño that is green when it is smoked.

POD DESCRIPTION

This depends on the Jalapeño variety used but the Chipotle Grande can be up to 15cm long.

GROWING INFO

Start by growing Jalapeños (see page 60).

SEED SUPPLIERS

See Jalapeños (page 60)

AKA

Chile Ahumado, Chile Meco, Chile Morita, Chile Navideño, Chile Típico.

# 32

# NuMex Sunrise, Sunset & Eclipse

SPECIES

*C. annuum*

POD DESCRIPTION

The NuMex Sunrise turns a bright yellow, while the NuMex Sunset is orange and the NuMex Eclipse turns a deep brown. The pods are all the same shape and size, at about 10–15cm long and 2–3cm wide, with thin flesh, ideal for drying.

GROWING INFO

They like a sunny position and grow to about 60cm high and 45cm wide, so they can be placed in large pots as patio plants.

SEED SUPPLIERS

BPC, CSB, MWCH, NMSU, SLP

USAGE

Ornamentals that are also ideal for drying for chilli flakes and also good when pickled whole.

These three chillies. developed at the New Mexico Agricultural Experiment Station by Paul W. Bosland, Jaime Iglesias and Steve D. Tanksley, were all developed from the same parents and are a cross between the Permagreen bell pepper and the New Mexico 6–4 (which produces pods that are 12–20cm long).

They were grown as ornamentals for use in colourful chilli *ristras* (strings of chillies) which are very popular in New Mexico and as souvenirs for tourists. Don't be put off by the ornamental tag as these three can also be used in cooking. They make the most interesting pickled chillies when combined whole in jars (do make sure to prick some holes in the pods with a cocktail stick before pickling to let the pickling mix enter the chillies). Once dried, you can crush them to make tricoloured chilli flakes.

SCOVILLE RATING

3,000–5,000 SHU

# 33

# Ací Sivri Pepper

SPECIES
.......................................
*C. annuum*

SCOVILLE
RATING

5,000–30,000
SHU

The Acı Sivri Pepper is of Turkish origin. It is a Cayenne-style chilli pepper (see page 96) and produces long, slender pods; they tend to curl a little as they grow.

The pods mature to a deep red colour but start as a yellowish green and the longer they mature the hotter they get. An excellent tip if the season has ended and you still have many green pods left is to deseed and pickle them in vinegar with a few spices.

This pepper is often listed as an heirloom variety (see page 8). It grows up to 90cm high and is a good producer of pods, with as many as 50 per plant.

### POD DESCRIPTION

**Long, slender pods growing to 22cm long and 1.5–2cm wide. Pods start a yellow-green colour and mature to dark red.**

### GROWING INFO

**Will need some space as they grow to 90cm high and will need support when fully mature.**

### SEED SUPPLIERS

**BS, PBPC, SLP**

### USAGE

**Being thin fleshed, they dry well, but are also excellent pickled when green.**

# 34 Fish Pepper

SPECIES

*C. annuum*

POD DESCRIPTION

The pods are almost white, become green with variegated white streaks which turn orange and brown and, finally, the whole pod turns red. They grow to 3–5cm long and 1–2cm wide, and have a blunt, rounded tip.

GROWING INFO

They grow well in growbags in a greenhouse to about 60cm high, but, as with most things grown this way, they need support as the shallow depth of compost does not give much support to the root system.

SEED SUPPLIERS

BPC, CH, CSB, HS, LS, SLP, VNG

This African American heirloom variety (see page 8) is believed to have started as a natural mutation of the Serrano pepper (see page 88).

The pods start almost white, before becoming green with variegated white streaks which develop to orange and brown. Finally, the whole pod turns red when fully mature. Not only the pods, but also the leaves and the stems of the pods, are variegated, making this a very pretty plant. It can be easily grown in containers as the plants are compact and grow to about 60cm high.

Why this chilli mutation has survived is probably down to the fact that in its immature state, when it is almost white, it can be added to a white sauce or a chowder as a hidden heat.

Remember, while the pod looks most interesting in the variegated white and green stage, any saved seeds will only be viable once the pods have fully matured to red.

Seeds are becoming commercially available, but were almost unheard of just a few years ago outside the Philadelphia/Baltimore region of the USA.

SCOVILLE RATING

5,000–30,000 SHU

# 35 NuMex Mirasol

SPECIES

*C. annuum*

POD DESCRIPTION

The pods start green and ripen to a bright red and, at 5cm long and 2cm wide, they make a great display.

GROWING INFO

This is a good compromise chilli plant when you have little space and need something that not only looks good, but can be used as well.

SEED SUPPLIERS

CCN, MWCH, PSEU, SLP, TCPC

USAGE

While considered an ornamental chilli, the plants being small and bushy, they are in fact a very usable chilli in cooking and are ideal for making into flakes or chilli powders.

This is another chilli where the pods point upwards, 'Mirasol' being Spanish for 'looking at the sun'. This variety was developed at the New Mexico Agricultural Experiment Station by Paul W. Bosland and Max M. Gonzalez and released in 1993/4 to fit a special niche in the market for a chilli plant that could be used to create decorative chilli wreathes (*ristras*) and for flower arranging. Ristras need to have leaves and pods together to give a good contrast. This plant produces clusters of long, thin-fleshed, conical pods that dry well and retain their colour.

This variety was developed by crossing the Santaka chilli and the La Blanca and then stabilizing the variety over seven generations.

SCOVILLE RATING

5,000–30,000 SHU

# 36 Aleppo Pepper

SPECIES

*C. annuum*

POD DESCRIPTION

The pods ripen to dark red and grow to about 10cm long and 2–3cm wide, slightly tapering to a blunt end.

GROWING INFO

A good, sturdy plant, but will need support and space to grow.

SEED SUPPLIERS

BPC, CCN, PBPC

AKA

Halab Pepper ('Halab' is the Arabic name for Aleppo), Halaby Pepper.

USAGE

Usually sold sun-dried, crushed and mixed with salt and olive oil.

The Aleppo Pepper is named after a city in northern Syria. One of the largest citites in the country, Aleppo was once known for being on the Silk Road, which extended 6,400km from China to the edge of Europe.

Traditionally, this pepper is sun-dried, deseeded, crushed, and mixed with salt and olive oil, and it is in this form that it is mostly available from specialist retailers. A store-cupboard staple for when things need a lift, it also makes a great flavouring for soups and stuffing mixes.

Seeds are becoming available so you can grow this at home.

SCOVILLE RATING

approx. 8,000– 12,000 SHU

# 37 NuMex Heritage Big Jim

**SPECIES**

*C. annuum*

**POD DESCRIPTION**

Pods have thick flesh and are 15–20cm in length.

**GROWING INFO**

I had great success with these a few years ago, setting the propagator to 18–20°C and the seeds sprouted within a few days. They like daytime temperatures above 17°C. The plants can grow to 1m high and 50cm around, so they will need a bit of space to grow.

**SEED SUPPLIERS**

BS, CH, CSB, CSU, LS, NN, NMSU, PBPC, PZW, SDCF, SLP, VNG

**SCOVILLE RATING**

7,000–9,000 SHU

The original NuMex Big Jim is listed in *The Guinness Book of Records* as having the world's largest chilli pods at 33.75cm, but over the years this New Mexican-style chilli was starting to show losses in yield and heat as well as other significant growing characteristics.

So the New Mexico State University Chile Pepper Breeding and Genetics Program set about returning this variety to its original specification, if not improving it a little. This process took almost ten years from obtaining a 200-seed sample from the Plant Germplasm Preservation Research Unit, where the original seeds had been preserved, to 2007, when they had established a new superior chilli, which was released as the NuMex Heritage Big Jim.

The process involved growing plants for seeds in controlled, insect-free conditions and then selecting just the plants that met the required criteria, doing this again and again, increasing the number of plants and those selected, until a stable variety was produced.

This new chilli variety maintained the virtues that made the original Big Jim so popular, but was much better suited to commercial growing, being more uniform in the plant's height and width and its maturity date.

The new Big Jim produced an increased yield of about 11 per cent on average. The heat increased to 9,000 SHU while retaining the required flavour profile.

# 38 Serrano

SPECIES

*C. annuum*

SCOVILLE
RATING

10,000–30,000
SHU

These little, bullet-shaped chillies are one of my favourites. They have a thin skin but thick, crunchy flesh, making them great chillies to use in a fresh salsa. I like to roast some ripe red ones on the barbecue before I start cooking the meat, then finely chop them and add them to my tomato salsa.

The Serrano originates from the Sierra mountains of Mexico and its name means from the *sierras* (mountains). The plants can grow to 70–90cm high.

If you have lots of green Serranos, use them to make a simple salsa verde. Remove the stalks from 10–20 green Serranos, roughly chop 5–6 green tomatoes, a large bunch of fresh coriander and a large, mild onion and add to a blender or food processor with 2 cloves of garlic. Blitz to an almost liquid consistency, adding a little salt to taste, if needed. Do feel free to adapt the recipe. I use green tomatoes as I always seem to have some about at that time of year, but for a real authentic salsa verde you would use tomatillos.

There are a number of interesting varieties of Serrano, including the Serrano Tampiqueno, which produces much larger pods, and the faster-maturing and milder F1 hybrid (see page 9), the Serrano del Sol, which is my favourite to grow.

## POD DESCRIPTION

The pods grow to 5–7cm long and 2–3cm in diameter.

## GROWING INFO

They can be grown in large pots. Oddly, I have found these grow better when you keep a few of them together. They will produce over 50 pods if you get the conditions right.

## SEED SUPPLIERS

BCS, CB, CF, CH, HS, LS, MWCH, NMSU, NN, PSEU, PZW, RFC, SDCF, SLP, SS, TCPC, TF, TWF, VNG

# 39   De Arbol

SPECIES
·················································

*C. annuum*

SCOVILLE
RATING
··············

15,000–30,000
SHU

These long, slender chillies from Mexico can grow to up to 10cm long. They look much like the Cayenne varieties (see page 96) but the flavour is quite different. The De Arbol is a more nutty, smoky flavour without the peppery hints of a Cayenne and you will see the De Arbol listed in many seed catalogues as a heritage or a heirloom variety (see page 8).

De Arbol means 'tree-like' in Spanish, which describes the way the plant grows, as it can easily reach 1.2m high and has long, stick-like stems.

I find this chilli's flavour is at its best after it has been dried, which helps to intensify the flavour. Once dried, the pods can be deseeded and ground to make a powder or flakes. If you are using them whole, open them up, remove the seeds and then lightly dry-fry them to help release the oils and aroma.

Most chillies darken when dehydrated and some thin-skinned varieties become semi-translucent. The De Arbol, in contrast, seems to retain its bright red colour. When buying dried, always pick the brightest-looking, as they darken with age.

## POD DESCRIPTION

**These are long, slender, thin-fleshed chillies which can have small undulations or constrictions in the flesh. They grow to 5–7cm long and 0.5–1cm wide. When fully ripe, they are a deep red with smooth, shiny skin.**

## GROWING INFO

**Can take a while to germinate. It is a bushy plant and will require some support as it can produce a very heavy crop. It likes a position in full sun.**

## SEED SUPPLIERS

**BPC, BS, HS, LS, NMSU, SLP**

## AKA

**Bird's Beak chilli (Pico de Pajaro) and the Rat's Tail chilli (Cola de Rata) because of the long, slender shape of the pods.**

## USAGE

**Dry and grind to make powder or flakes or lightly dry-fry whole.**

# 40 Facing Heaven

SPECIES
.............................................
*C. annuum*

SCOVILLE
RATING
..........................
15,000–30,000
SHU

The Facing Heaven chilli gets its name from the way the pods point upwards. They have become well known through their use in Sichuan cuisine, where they are used whole in great quantities to add flavour to dishes, but you are not expected to eat the chillies unless you want to.

The pods start green and turn bright red, making this a most ornamental-looking plant. There are a number of varieties, from long, slender pods to round, cone-shaped ones. My favourites are the cone shaped ones, as they have a strong lemony citrus flavour and vibrant red colour.

The dried pods are most often used whole at the start of cooking, dry-fried or fried in a little oil to release their flavour. One of my favourite dishes using these chillies is Sichuan hot pot, which includes fresh ginger, Sichuan pepper and Facing Heaven chillies.

## POD DESCRIPTION

The pods start green and turn red, vary in shape, depending on the variety, are thin skinned and grow to 3–6cm long and 1–2cm in diameter.

## GROWING INFO

A short, bushy plant that produces lots of pods. I saved seeds from pods purchased in an oriental supermarket, but very few germinated.

## SEED SUPPLIERS

BS, CH, LS

## AKA

Chao Tian Jiao, Heaven Chile, Liuzhou.

## USAGE

They are easy to dehydrate at home using a dehydrator and are also very good when used to make chilli oil.

# 41 Manzano

*C. pubescens*

SCOVILLE
RATING

15,000–30,000
SHU

The Manzano, AKA Rocoto, comes from a species of chillies called *Capsicum pubescens* (see page 7).

While counted as a domesticated variety, it is one of the rarest, coming from Peru in the western South America, where it is able to grow in cooler climatic conditions than most chillies. Unfortunately, it is still not frost resistant. It can be grown for a number of years, the plant becoming almost a small chilli tree in appearance.

'Manzano' means 'apple', and these pods do look like small, round apples. They have very thick flesh and skin, making them hard to dehydrate, so they are normally used fresh.

A bit of an oddity is the Rocoto San Isidro, which is linked to the small village of San Isidro where it is said to be grown by a priest in the grounds of the church. San Isidro is on the island of La Palma on the Canary Islands. This is a long way from the forests of Peru and how it got there is unknown.

## POD DESCRIPTION

Small, round pods grow up to 5cm in diameter. The pods can be a little elongated, like a plum tomato. They are available in a range of colours, including red, green, orange and yellow.

## GROWING INFO

These can be a little harder to grow and do not like direct sunlight, but prefer the shade of other plants. In particularly warm summers in cool-temperate areas as well as in warmer climates, they will happily grow outside in large pots, but will need support as they can reach 2m high.

## SEED SUPPLIERS

BPC, CCN, CF, CH, MWCH, NN, PSEU, RFC, SLP, TF

## USAGE

Use fresh to make a great, fruity base for a salsa or chutney. With their round shape and thick flesh they would also be good with the stem and seeds removed, and then pickled or stuffed and roasted as with the Peruvian dish Rocoto Relleno.

# 42 Cayenne Pepper

*C. annuum, C.
frutescens*

SCOVILLE
RATING

15,000–50,000
SHU

The Cayenne pepper gets its name from the city of Cayenne in French Guiana. It is a very popular pepper and all supermarkets and grocers will have some form of it on sale.

It has also become synonymous with the medical uses of peppers. Cayenne has been recommended for everything from coughs, ulcers and sore throats to the prevention of heart attacks and strokes. Some research has shown it can dissolve fibrin, a protein used in the formation of blood clots, and may also stop plaque forming on the walls of arteries.

The diet industry has also started to catch on to its magical properties and it has been used as an appetite suppressor and may help with weight loss as it raises body temperature, burning more energy and speeding up metabolism.

Cayenne is not a single variety of chilli pepper, but a collection of chilli varieties that share a common style and flavour. I have seen it described as both *Capsicum frutescens* and *C. annuum* but most seed catalogues come down on the *C. annuum* side.

## POD DESCRIPTION

A long, slender pod that starts green and ripens to red. It can grow to 30cm long, in the case of Joe's Long Cayenne (see page 102), but most varieties are much shorter: 5–12cm. They do not usually exceed 1cm wide and all taper to a sharp point.

## GROWING INFO

To germinate set your propagator to 20°C and the seed should sprout in 5–10 days. Cayenne plants like space for their roots, but will grow well in larger pots.

## SEED SUPPLIERS

BPC, BS, CF, CH, CSB, HS, NN, PZW, SLP, SS, UKCS, VNG

## AKA

African Pepper, Bird Pepper, Cockspur Pepper, Cow Horn Pepper, Devil's Tongue, Goat's Pepper, Guinea Pepper, Hot Flame, Red Bird Pepper.

## USAGE

Has medical and weight-reduction, as well as culinary, uses.

# 43 Criolla Sella

SPECIES

*C. baccatum*

POD DESCRIPTION

The pods start green and mature to a golden orange, 4–6cm in length and 1–1.5cm wide, with a slender, cylindrical shape.

GROWING INFO

There are no real problems growing the Criolla Sella. It is known for being one of the best to overwinter but is not frost resistant, so in cool-temperate climates bring inside before it gets too cold.

SEED SUPPLIERS

BPC, CCN, PBPC, SLP

USAGE

Eat as they are, freshly picked, use to make salsa or a sauce or dry to make chilli powder.

This is a great little plant from Bolivia in South America. Short, strong and sturdy, and it needs to be, since it is generally heavily covered in pods. A great plus for this variety is that it matures early and is suited to cool-temperate climates. Being compact, it can be grown in large pots in a conservatory or greenhouse and moved outside once the weather is warmer.

The Wiltshire Chilli Farm in the UK used them to make a single-variety sauce that really showed off this chilli's unique flavour. It combined some cider vinegar and orange juice with just a few spices to make this sauce.

Criolla Sella chillies have a delightful citrus flavour and are mild enough to be munched straight from the plant or, my favourite, sliced and added to a cheese sandwich.

The thin skins make them ideal for drying as they make an excellent, slightly sweet chilli powder, but also work well fresh in a salsa or a sauce.

SCOVILLE
UNITS

20,000–30,000
SHU

# 44 Black Pearl

SPECIES

*C. annuum*

POD DESCRIPTION

The pods are round
and about 1–2.5cm in
diameter. Dark purple
pods ripen to red.

GROWING INFO

These like the sun, and
are great when grown in
large pots on the patio.

SEED SUPPLIERS

CF, CH, HS, NN, SLP,
UKCS

USAGE

Generally grown as an
ornamental.

This chilli is described as an ornamental and
is a great-looking plant, but don't let the word
'ornamental' put you off, as all peppers are edible.
It has dark, almost black, leaves and bunches
of round pods (black pearls), that poke upright
through the foliage, and which uniquely start as
dark purple and finally ripen to red.

Black Pearl has nothing to do with pirate
films; it was developed by plant geneticist
John Stommel (ARS Vegetable Laboratory)
and Robert Griesbach (ARS Floral & Nursery
Plant Research Unit), in conjunction with
PanAmerican Seeds and McCorkle Nurseries.
Released in 2005, it was a winner of an All-
American Selections (AAS) award, recognizing
its improved qualities, in 2006.

It is an ideal pepper for planting in large
containers on a patio since it only grows to 50cm
high and 40cm wide, and, as peppers go, it has
the looks to die for.

SCOVILLE
RATING

25,000–30,000
SHU

# 45 Joe's Long Cayenne

SPECIES

*C. annuum*

POD DESCRIPTION

Long pods, often of more than 30cm.

GROWING INFO

A productive and fun chilli to grow, it will need support as it develops owing to the weight of the pods.

SEED SUPPLIERS

BPC, CH, NN, PJ, PSEU, PZW, SS, SSS, VNG

AKA

Pinocchio's Nose, Whippet's Tail.

USAGE

Ideal for drying.

Cayenne chillies normally produce long, thin pods that taper to a point with thin flesh, but the Joe's Long Cayenne does have an extreme talent for producing long pods, the length often exceeding 30cm.

I have been told by seed companies how easily chilli varieties can multiply. This chilli is a case in point. In the early 1990s, Peppers by Post, a British mail order fresh chilli business, wanted to offer a cayenne with a difference, so looked at American seed companies and discovered Joe's Long Cayenne. As the variety was unknown in the UK at that time, and they did not want to give their secret variety away, they called the pods they were selling 'Whippet's Tail'.

They never changed the name of a variety but, as they were selling this as a pod and not as seed, this was deemed acceptable practice. However, within a very few years, they started seeing 'Whippet's Tail' seeds being offered for sale, and you can still see these on the internet today.

At this time, they worked with Tozers Seed Company and showed the Joe's Long Cayenne plants to them. Tozers purchased seed and, in turn, offered it to Thompson & Morgan seed company for retail sales. However, for their retail packs, Thompson & Morgan called the seed 'Pinocchio's Nose' and this was how one chilli became three.

At a recent chilli display at West Dean Gardens, near Chichester, UK, there were three identical plants. They were labelled: Joe's Long Cayenne, Whippet's Tail and Pinocchio's Nose.

SCOVILLE RATING

20,000–50,000 SHU

# 46 Peter Pepper

SPECIES

*C. annuum*

POD DESCRIPTION

The pods grow to 7.5–
10cm long and 2–3cm
wide and ripen from
green to red. Other
colours are becoming
available, with both
yellow and orange
varieties listed in
some of the online seed
catalogues.

GROWING INFO

Easy to grow in a grow-
bag. In cool-temperate
climates, the plants like
to be in a greenhouse or
a sunny conservatory.

SEED SUPPLIERS

BPC, CF, HS, LS,
MWCH, NN, PJ, PSEU,
RFC, SLP, TCPC, TF,
TWF, VNG

AKA

Chilli Willy, Penis
Pepper.

USAGE

Mainly an ornamental,
although also grown on
a commercial basis for
use in hot sauces. Use
in fresh salsas.

Are these the peppers Peter Piper picked?
Probably not.

The Peter Pepper had to be included, just
because of its alternate names, Penis Pepper or
Chilli Willy. As you can probably see from the
picture, these have an unusual phallic shape that,
when ripe, resembles the human penis.

Originating from Louisiana and Texas, USA,
this pepper is now most commonly grown as an
ornamental, because of the shape of the pod,
but it has also been grown on a limited scale
commercially for use in hot sauces.

Described as an heirloom variety (see page
8), this pepper has only survived as it has some
culinary use. Luckily, it does taste pretty good.
Just think of the recipes you can make and name
inappropriately, using this chilli…

For Peter's penis pepper salsa – a simple, fresh
salsa – roughly chop 3–4 ripe tomatoes and add
to a blender or food processor with 2–3 peeled
and chopped garlic cloves, 1 chopped onion and
3–4 chopped fresh Peter Peppers. Blend to a
smooth consistency. Pour the mixture into a bowl
and add 3–4 chopped ripe tomatoes (to give your
salsa a chunkier texture), 3 tablespoons chopped
fresh coriander and lime juice to taste. Season
with salt and pepper, mix thoroughly and serve
with tortilla chips.

SCOVILLE
RATING

25,000–35,000
SHU

# 47 Poinsettia

With its mass of dark green leaves and clusters of bright red chilli pods pointing up, the Poinsettia chilli has a striking resemblance to the well-known Poinsettia plant.

Normally grown as an ornamental, this chilli does produce a mass of pods which are very useable in the kitchen. They are best used with the seeds removed as there are a lot of them for a pod of this size.

Poinsettia is very similar to, and maybe the same as, the Takanotsume chilli from Japan, which is also known as the Hawk's Claw Pepper because of its curved, talon-like shape. The Takanotsume and the Yatsufusa chillies (see page 110) are dried and used as the main ingredients of Shichimi tōgarashi.

Poinsettias are also ideal for drying and using to make chilli flakes. Chop off the stem and calyx, split the pods lengthways and place them in a dehydrator.

SCOVILLE RATING

25,000–40,000
SHU

# 48 Shata Baladi

SPECIES

*C. annuum*

POD DESCRIPTION

The skyward-pointing,
erect, green pods droop
down as they enlarge
and ripen from green
through black/purple
to a bright red. They can
grow to 4–7cm long and
2–3cm wide and can have
an almost plum-tomato
shape.

GROWING INFO

It is a beautiful-looking,
bushy plant which can
grow to 70cm high. It can
be grown in large pots or
containers, but will need
a bit of warmth and sun
to get the maximum out
of the plants.

SEED SUPPLIERS

SLP

USAGE

Generally grown as an
ornamental.

From Egypt comes the Shata Baladi, which
produces a multitude of pods. With thick skins
and a slight sweet and fruity flavour, these chillies
are excellent dried and ground into a mild to
warm paprika. You will probably need to use a
dehydrator because of the thick flesh of these
pods, but it is worth it as they retain their colour
well. If you are going to make powder or flakes,
cut the pods in half from top to bottom, to aid the
drying. The aroma as they dry is wonderful.

The seeds of this variety are not the easiest
seed to find, but a search of some of the chilli-
growing forums should find some seeds if you
cannot source any from the chilli seed specialists.

SCOVILLE
RATING

25,000–50,000
SHU

# 49 Yatsafusa

SPECIES

*C. annuum*

POD DESCRIPTION

Long, slender pods grow
upright in clusters of 5–6
pods from the top of each
branch.

GROWING INFO

A beautiful-looking,
compact plant, ideal for
large pots on a sunny
patio.

SEED SUPPLIERS

NMSU, PBPC, PJ, PSEU

AKA

Hontaka, Japones,
Santaka.

USAGE

Like other Cayenne-style
peppers, it is a good
variety to dehydrate
and can then provide
heat and flavour all year
around. When dried, it
is a main ingredient of
Shichimi tōgarashi.

This is the Japanese equivalent of the Cayenne
(see page 96), but it is better known in the west
as the Japones.

This beautiful plant is a small, compact
variety. The name 'Yatsafusa', when referring
to trees, means 'dwarf' and this chilli grows to
45–60cm high, making it ideal for growing in
pots on a balcony or other confined space.

Yatsafusa is a key part of Sichuan cuisine and
you can easily make a Sichuan-style chilli oil
using last year's dried pods. Finely chop about
8–10 dried pods and place them in a heatproof
glass container. In a small frying pan, heat about
200ml oil (not olive oil in this case, as you will
need an oil that can take the heat) until it starts
to smoke. Remove from the heat, let it cool for a
minute or two and then carefully pour it over the
chopped chillies. Cover and leave to cool and,
once cooled, strain out the chillies.

Both the Yatsafusa and the Takanotsume
chillies are dried and used as the main
ingredients of Shichimi tōgarashi, a blend of
spices and seasoning that is used as a table
condiment for soups and noodles.

SCOVILLE
RATING

25,000–75,000
SHU

# 50

# Demon Red

SPECIES

*C.annuum*

POD DESCRIPTION

Smooth-skinned pods
grow to 2–4cm long and
up to 0.5cm wide and
ripen from green to red.

GROWING INFO

Easy to grow, they will
reach a maximum of
around 35cm around.
Grow in a smallish pot
and leave it out on the
patio during hot summer
days. This variety is not
very tolerant of colder
climates, but it is happy
to grow indoors in a
sunny position.

SEED SUPPLIERS

BS, NN, SLP, TCPC,
VNG

This small, compact, ornamental chilli has been
bred to grow in small containers and is great for
the windowsill. It produces a mass of upward-
facing small pods that start green and ripen to
a fiery red.

While described as ornamental, these little
pods, 2–4cm long and up to 0.5cm wide, are very
edible and ideally suited to Thai cooking. Like
many ornamentals these can taste a little bitter,
but they have a pleasant Cayenne-style peppery
flavour (see page 96).

A past winner of an RHS Award of Garden
Merit, they are easy to grow. Pick them direct
from the plant as you need them, but once the
weather starts to cool down pick your remaining
pods and let them dry. As they are thin fleshed
they will dry easily and keep you warm till the
next season's crop is ready.

SCOVILLE
RATING

30,000–50,000 SHU

# 51 Diavolilli

## SPECIES

*C. annuum*

## POD DESCRIPTION

Ripens from dark green
to bright red, reaching
3.5cm long and 6mm
wide.

## GROWING INFO

Nice, compact plant,
easily grown but
will probably need a
greenhouse in cool-
temperate areas if it is to
reach its full potential.

## SEED SUPPLIERS

No commercial seed
supplier has been found,
so you may have to search
seed exchange websites
and forums.

## AKA

In Italy they are also
known as Diavolicchio
(Little Devil) chilli or
Pellegrino (Pilgrim)
chilli.

## USAGE

Try finely sliced and
fried in a little olive oil,
then tossed through
fresh pasta.

This is a compact, bush-like chilli plant that
grows to 50cm high and the same wide, with the
pods pointing up though the foliage.

The Diavolilli chilli originates from Calabria/
Basilicata in southern Italy, where it is the chilli
used in the chilli-eating competition at the
Annual Diamante Peperoncino Festival. The
competition entails eating as many 50-gram
plates of the chillies as possible in 30 minutes.

Sometimes you can find this variety powdered
or dried in specialist shops.

SCOVILLE
RATING

30,000–50,000
SHU

# 52 Ají Amarillo

SCOVILLE
RATING
.....................................
30,000–50,000
SHU

'Amarillo' translates as 'yellow' and 'ají' means 'chilli' in Spanish. This chilli starts green and ripens to a deep orange and its thick flesh has fruity flavour.

Outside of Peru and Bolivia, they can be found dried whole or as powder, when they can also be called Ají Mirasol or Cusqueno. If you buy them dried, they can be rehydrated in a little warm water for 15–20 minutes, while the powdered form is often used to flavour or colour rice.

Ají Amarillo are a staple of Peruvian cuisine and very versatile. Try rehydrating them, then blend to a fine paste and use them to flavour home-made mayonnaise. If you are more adventurous, then a quick search of the internet will find recipes such as Causa Rellena (a potato and chicken salad), Papas a la Huancaína (potato in a white cheese sauce) and Ají de Gallina (chicken in a spicy cream sauce).

### POD DESCRIPTION

Pods start green and ripen to deep orange and they grow to 10–15cm long.

### GROWING INFO

Plants can grow to well over 1m high. To germinate the seeds they need a temperature above 18°C. The plants enjoy full sun but need to be kept watered, and in cool-temperate climates, they will happily grow in a sunny conservatory or greenhouse.

### SEED SUPPLIERS

CH, HS, LS, NN, SLP

### AKA

Ají Escabeche, Ají Mirasol (dried), Cusqueno (dried), Peruvian chilli.

### USAGE

There are a number of commercial sauces available that are made with this chilli.

# 53 Bangalore Torpedo

SPECIES

*C. frutescens*

POD DESCRIPTION

The pods grow to about 13cm long and 1cm wide, maturing from light green to bright red.

GROWING INFO

Will need some space, as plants tend to spread out unless trained.

SEED SUPPLIERS

HS, SS

USAGE

The pods are ideal for pickling when green, when they are milder, and for drying when mature. This chilli is great for clearing sinuses.

The 3-m long Bangalore Torpedo developed in 1912 by the British Indian Army was used to clear mines. Unfortunately, this was not a chilli plant! The plant is a long, slender Cayenne-style chilli (see page 96) and is used in Indian cuisine.

This Indian chilli matures from a light green colour to a bright red and can tend to curve and twist a little. The plant grows to 1m high.

These are great pickled. You will want to wash the chillies well and prick a few holes in the flesh to let the pickling liquor do its work. Pack as many as you can into a tall, sterilized jar so you can later pull out individual chillies and then make the pickling liquor with 500ml water, 500ml distilled white vinegar and 2 teaspoons non-iodized salt.

Place all the ingredients in a pan and bring to the boil. Leave to cool for 10–15 minutes and then pour slowly into the jar of chillies until they are all covered, carefully tapping the jar to release any air bubbles.

Seal the jar with a tight lid and the pickled chillies should be ready to eat in a couple of weeks. They will keep, unopened, for up to a year. Once opened, store in the refrigerator.

SCOVILLE RATING

30,000–50,000 SHU

# 54 NuMex Twilight

## SPECIES

*C. annuum*

## POD DESCRIPTION

The 2cm-long, upright pods ripen from purple, through to yellow, orange and red.

## GROWING INFO

An excellent and simple variety to grow and an ideal gift; it is hard to kill and looks great. The plants grow upright, though the main stem is strong and does not need staking. Provided they are grown in full light, plants will become bushy. They perform well in small pots, adapting their size to fill the pot.

## SEED SUPPLIERS

BS, CB, CCN, CSB, HS, LS, MWCH, NN, PSEU, SDCF, SLP, SS, SSS, TCPC, TF, TWF, VNG

## USAGE

Ideal as a house plant.

This may be the ultimate potted plant chilli, as it is one of the prettiest. With the upright fruit starting purple, then ripening to a yellow, orange and red, the pods provide a more colourful display than any flowering plant. The fruiting season starts in early summer and continues right up to early winter, giving a beautiful display for a very long time.

The seed is a good germinator and the plants grow easily, so, along with Super Chile F1 and Super Tramp (see page 134), NuMex Twilight is one of the easiest chilli varieties to grow and suitable for beginners to try.

An alternative is a variety called Fairy Lights, which is best described as a cousin of the NuMex Twilight, except that its stems are dark purple, the leaves have an attractive purpling over them and the flowers are fully purple.

You may well find either of these being sold by your local garden centre since they are both very popular varieties.

SCOVILLE RATING

30,000–50,000 SHU

# 55 Pusa Jwala

SPECIES

*C. annuum*

POD DESCRIPTION

Pods grow to 8–14cm long and ripen from light green to orange and finally red.

GROWING INFO

Designed for commercial growing, this variety needs space to develop. It is not hard to grow, but its size means it is not recommended for the home grower. If you do want to try them, I have found it best to soak the seeds for a few days before placing them in a warm place or at 20°C in a seed propagator. In cool-temperate climates, they will need a large polytunnel.

SEED SUPPLIERS

BCS, BPC, HS, NN, PSEU, PZW

USAGE

In India pods are used green to make curries and chutneys when fresh and, once ripe, they are dried and processed into chilli powder.

This was developed from the cross-breeding of two other Indian chilli varieties, NP 46A and the Puri Red. These long, wrinkled chillies are one of the most popular commercial varieties grown in Andhra Pradesh, one of India's major chilli-growing areas.

The plants can be over 1m high and produce a large crop of pods. In cool-temperate climates, these need to be grown in a polytunnel and, unless you have a very large polytunnel, I do not recommend trying to grow these at home. Instead, look out for them dried or fresh at Indian supermarkets.

If you do want to grow some Pusa Jwala, the dried pods are a great source of seeds. Seeds collected in this way are not always the most viable as they have probably not been stored in ideal conditions, but you will get lots of seeds to try to germinate and you only need a few to grow.

SCOVILLE RATING

30,000–50,000 SHU

# 56

# Sibirischer Haus Paprika

SPECIES

*C. annuum*

POD DESCRIPTION

Erect, skyward-pointing, short, 2.5 ×
1.5cm blunt-ended pods
that mature from dark
green to red.

GROWING INFO

The ideal indoor pot
plant; move it outside
in the summer and it
should last many years.

SEED SUPPLIERS

SLP

USAGE

Dried and ground to
powder.

This is a very fast-producing variety and a rarity
outside Siberia. The name translates as 'Siberian
house pepper'. The variety has been developed to
produce peppers in poor light conditions and is
less susceptible in cool conditions.

The compact plant produces an abundance of
pods. Siberia has little in the way of commercial
chilli development so I suspect this has been
evolved as growers have selected the seeds from
successful plants and passed these on to other
growers, who have in turn done the same.

Sibirscher Haus Paprika makes an ideal
pot plant and will be happy on a windowsill
not in direct sunlight. It is reported that they
overwinter well and can last many years.

When dried and ground to a powder, they are
used in local dishes such as *Gulaš* (goulash) or
*Perkelt*, a pork and paprika stew.

SCOVILLE
UNITS

30,000–50,000
SHU

# 57 Tabasco

SPECIES

*C. frutescens*

SCOVILLE
RATING

30,000–50,000
SHU

This chilli gets its name from the Mexican state of Tabasco, and has been made famous as the main ingredient in Tabasco Pepper Sauce, probably the best-known chilli sauce in the world.

The production of Tabasco Pepper Sauce dates back to 1868, when Edmund McIlhenny started selling his sauce to the public. The sauce was based on his locally grown Tabasco chillies, which are picked when ripe and ground to a pepper mash before having salt added and then sealed in oak barrels to mature. The maturing process can take up to three years, then the Tabasco mash is combined with vinegar before finally being bottled and sold.

If you are growing these and don't want to emulate Edmund McIlhenny, then use them to make a great fresh salsa. Just deseed and then finely chop up 4–5 ripe Tabasco pods and add to some chopped fresh tomatoes, about 8–10 should do. Then add a chopped sweet pepper, a crushed clove of garlic and the juice of a lime. Finally add some chopped fresh coriander and a little salt and pepper to taste, and you will have a simple, tasty salsa in just a few minutes.

## POD DESCRIPTION

The conical, upward-pointing pods will grow to around 5cm long and 1–1.5cm wide, maturing from green through yellow to red. They can be used at any stage, but it is traditional to wait for the pods to turn red and this also is when they are at their best both for flavour and heat.

## GROWING INFO

A very popular chilli to grow, seeds are available almost everywhere. The plant likes a good sunny position and a moist soil; watering every other day should be sufficient. If conditions are right, it can produce a heavy crop of pods.

## SEED SUPPLIERS

BCS, BPC, BS, CCN, CH, CSB, HS, LS, NMSU, NN, PBPC, PSEU, PZW, SLP, SS, SSS, TCPC, TF, TWF, VNG

## USAGE

The main ingredient in Tabasco Pepper Sauce.

# 58 Dundicut

SPECIES

*C. annuum*

POD DESCRIPTION

The small, round to almost teardrop-shaped pods are 1.5–2.5cm in diameter.

GROWING INFO

In a warm and sunny environment, plants should not be hard to grow.

SEED SUPPLIERS

PBPC, SLP

AKA

Lar Mirch

USAGE

Used to make chilli powder.

Apparently the Dundicut is the national pepper of Pakistan – so important is it to the national cuisine – but it seems it has not yet made it to the growing list of producers in other countries. Pakistan is one of the world's largest producers of chillies with an annual production of 100,000 tons. It seems that this chilli is most commonly grown to make chilli powder, probably because of its bright red colour.

In countries other than Pakistan, you can find dried Dundicut chillies in specialist Pakistani shops and online at specialist spice companies. I have only seen them sold with the stem removed and, in fact, one supplier lists the Dundicut as meaning 'stemless', which may also be why they are popular to process to powder.

Seeds have not commonly been available but a few suppliers are now stocking them. If you can source any, try growing some to see what they taste like fresh. It is one I cannot wait to try.

SCOVILLE
RATING

30,000–65,000
SHU

# 59 Goat Horn Pepper

SPECIES

*C. annuum*

POD DESCRIPTION

The slender, tapering pods ripen from dark green to bright red and are 15cm long and 1.5cm wide.

GROWING INFO

Pods need time to ripen, so plants are best grown in a greenhouse or polytunnel in cool-temperate climates.

SEED SUPPLIERS

SS

USAGE

It is ideal for making a Thai green curry.

This chilli originates from Thailand. It is a nice, compact plant that can grow 60–90cm tall. In cool-temperate climates, it is best grown in a greenhouse or polytunnel as it is a bit of a late developer when it comes to getting the chillies fully ripe.

The long, tapering, slender pods are often described as a Cayenne-style as they share a similar shape, but not the distinct, black-pepper flavour of the Cayenne (see page 96).

Matt Simpson at Simpson's Seeds (see page 223) makes the sweet smoky Horny Goat Sauce using the Goat Horn Chilli. He describes the plant as a high-yielding chilli with a good flavour.

Note that there is also an Italian pepper from the Abruzzo region called the Corno Di Capra, or Goat Horn in English. This is a much more mild pepper, at around 2,000 SHU.

SCOVILLE RATING

35,000–50,000 SHU

# 60 Bacio di Satana

**SPECIES**

*C. annuum*

**POD DESCRIPTION**

The cherry-shaped pods grow to 2.5cm in diameter, starting lime-green and turning scarlet-red when mature.

**GROWING INFO**

This is a good chilli to grow, even for the novice. It grows to about 45cm high, likes full sun and would be ideal in a conservatory or greenhouse in cool-temperate climates. It produces a consistently high yield of pods.

**SEED SUPPLIERS**

NN

**AKA**

Ciliegia Piccante.

'Satan's kiss' is the best translation of Bacio di Satana I have come across. These little, cherry-shaped chillies originate from southern Italy.

The pods grow facing the sky, making a very interesting-looking display. They are thick fleshed and, with the stem and seeds removed, are ideal for stuffing. You may find them in Italian delicatessens stuffed with a mixture of tuna, anchovies and capers and then stored in olive oil.

I have used these to make chilli sherry. Many years ago, the late Peter Seymour (aka Chilli Pepper Pete) introduced me to his recipe, which, like most good ideas, is very simple, but tastes great. The sherry makes a great drink on cold winter days.

You will need a bottle or two of sherry. The better the sherry you use, the more drinkable it will be. You need to cut slits in the chillies to let the sherry in, then cover the chillies in sherry and store in an airtight container in the refrigerator for a few weeks. Then strain the sherry mixture back into the sterilized sherry bottles, saving the chillies to make a chilli mash, which you do by pushing the reserved chillies through a sieve to remove the seeds. Store the resulting mash in an airtight container in the refrigerator and use it to spice up stir-fries, etc.

SCOVILLE RATING

40,000–50,000 SHU

# 61

# Super Chile F1 & Super Tramp

## SPECIES

*C. annuum*

## POD DESCRIPTION

Pods 6–8cm long and 1.5cm wide and ripen from light green to red.

## GROWING INFO

My absolute first recommendation for the novice chilli grower, it is very easy to grow, produces excellent usable pods and is a reliable cropper. I grow mine on a sunny part of the patio in a grow-bag every year. You will not be disappointed.

## SEED SUPPLIERS

PSEU, SS, SSS, VNG

Super Chile has the appearance of what many people would consider to be an 'ordinary chilli', thus it is what people expect when they think 'chilli'. However, despite this, it has a place in any chilli grower's top ten list as it is truly an exceptional variety. The particular features that give it its elevated place are its earliness and reliability.

This is the variety recommended to beginners: it is a good germinator, forgiving in less than perfect conditions, fast growing, and will produce copious yields of hot pods.

Being an F1 hybrid variety from the USA, availability can be an issue to growers outside the USA.

A new variety called Super Tramp is a product of de-hybridizing (see page 8) Super Chile. Over many generations, this has been developed as an open-pollinated variety (see page 8) that has all the characteristics of Super Chile. It looks identical to Super Chile, has all the positive characteristics, but by not being an F1 hybrid, saved seeds, if not crossed with others, will remain true to the variety.

Note that the Super Chile variety was developed in the USA, hence the correct spelling of this variety is the American spelling 'chile', not 'chilli', but you will find it listed in seed catalogues under both names.

**SCOVILLE RATING**

40,000–50,000 SHU

# 62 Purple Haze

*C. annuum*

## POD DESCRIPTION

Cayenne-style pods (see page 96) are 7–8cm long and 1cm thin, tapering to a point. The pods turn from green to purple at an early stage. Even the stalks and calyces are purple and as the pods ripen they start to turn a dark red.

## GROWING INFO

Likes a large pot or to be grown in the ground. This is a sprawling plant that will need support once it starts to crop.

## SEED SUPPLIERS

CF, SSS

## USAGE

These are not the hottest chillis but try them in a salsa for an unusual colour combination. The full heat does not develop until they are ripe, but I like using them when they are purple, in chutneys and pickles. I have also dried them and they retain their colour well.

This plant is described as having an 'old-fashioned', open growth habit, which in layman's terms means it is not very compact and, having lots of branches, it is therefore not suitable for small pots as it needs room to grow. Having said that, it is a beautiful plant with lilac-purple flowers, leaves and stems.

If you have the space, this is an interesting variety to grow, just for the colour. Purple has become a very fashionable colour for vegetables and a quick search of the internet will turn up a carrot also called Purple Haze. There are even some claims that the purple colour in foods is good for your memory. I have just remembered that 1967 song by Jimi Hendrix, 'Purple Haze', so my memory is working.

SCOVILLE
RATING

50,000–75,000
SHU

# 63

# Cheiro Roxa

SPECIES

*C. chinense*

POD DESCRIPTION

The pods are 2.5cm in diameter and start dark purple and mature to lighter purple.

GROWING INFO

This unique looking chilli is easy to grow but can take a while to fully ripen.

SEED SUPPLIERS

CCN, NN, PBPC, SLP, UKCS, VNG

USAGE

Ideal for a chutney or pickle once deseeded (this may prove a little fiddly).

Coming from Brazil, the Cheiro Roxa ('Roxa' is Portuguese for 'purple') is a most unusual pepper, looking a little like the pod has been compressed so that the middle bulges out.

The pods start dark purple before ripening to a light purple, sometimes with even lighter pink streaks. The plants grow quite tall, up to 1m high, and have purplish green leaves. They crop well, producing lots of pods.

At 50,000–100,000 SHU, this is a hot variety and among that heat there is a little sweetness to the flavour.

SCOVILLE
RATING

50,000–100,000
SHU

# 64 Coffee Bean

This is another unusual Habanero variety and the original seeds are suspected to come from Central America. About 15 years ago some of these seeds came into the hands of Joy and Michael Michaud of Sea Spring Seeds, who grew them and named the chilli the Coffee Bean since when fully ripe the pods have the look of coffee berries.

The pods have a very noticeable fruity aroma which is matched by their flavour. The round pods grow to about 6–8mm in diameter, starting green before turning bright orange and then finally, when fully mature, they become shiny red.

If you are looking for a Wiri Wiri chilli then this makes a good, if a little milder, alternative. The pods are so small and compact that cutting them is not always a good option and Joy recommends just crushing them with the back of a knife when used in cooking.

I would try pickling some whole or adding them to some pickled onions to give a extra bite.

SCOVILLE
RATING

77,000 SHU

# 65

# Tepin & Pequin

SPECIES

*C. annuum*

POD DESCRIPTION

Tepin pods are small and berry-like at 5mm–1cm diameter; Pequin pods are slightly more elongated.

GROWING INFO

Both varieties can be hard to germinate and may require a long time in a warm propagator (25°C+) before they burst into life. Once growing they can reach 1–2m in height – not for the novice, but if you can get hold of some seeds give them a go. Tricks for success include slightly scarifying the seeds (cutting the seed coat to encourage germination) to replicate the conditions of being digested by a bird, or growing them in sandy, free-draining soil.

SEED SUPPLIERS

BPC, CF, CH, CSB, HS, LS, NMSU, PBPC, PZW, SLP, VNG

AKA

Bird Pepper

These are wild chillies (see page 7) that can be found in Mexico and the southern America states of Arizona, Texas and New Mexico. It is said that with the right conditions plants can live for up to 50 years.

The name 'Tepin' comes from the Nahuati (Aztec) Mexican word for 'flea', ideal for a very small chilli with such a big bite. The plant can produce an amazing number of pods, but these pods are very small and more like berries.

A very similar pepper called the Pequin (which means 'small' or 'tiny') is normally slightly more elongated than the round Tepin. Both these peppers probably share a common ancestry since they are both wild peppers and grow in the same regions. The Pequin grows wild but is often harvested, dried and then sold in the local markets. A few online stores can provide both seeds and pods.

These peppers may also be known as the Bird Peppers and, under this name, variants can be found as far south as Argentina and spreading into the West Indies.

SCOVILLE
RATING

50,000–250,000
SHU

# 66 Ají Cereza

SPECIES

*C. annuum*

POD DESCRIPTION

The pods are 2–3cm in diameter. They mature from green to red.

GROWING INFO

Can grow to 90cm high and needs warmth; grown in a polytunnel or greenhouse in cool-temperate climates.

SEED SUPPLIERS

PBPC, SLP

USAGE

Pods dry well and can be deseeded and pickled or stuffed with cheese and roasted.

'Cereza' is 'cherry' in Spanish and 'ají' means 'pepper' or 'chilli', so this variety translates as 'Cherry Pepper'. Ají Cereza is a small, roundish red pepper (much like a cherry!) from the jungles of Peru. The pods start green and mature to red and, being thin fleshed, they dry well. They are well packed with seeds and if you carefully cut out the stem and remove the seeds they can then be easily pickled or stuffed with cheese and roasted.

Ají Cereza are not normally grown commercially, but are available dried via specialist retailers, in which case they look like a smaller version of the Cascabel (see page 42), if a little lighter in colour and with a lot less heat.

SCOVILLE
RATING

60,000–80,000
SHU

# 67 Murupi Amarela

*C. chinense*

SCOVILLE
RATING

60,000–100,000
SHU

Coming from the north of Brazil is the Murupi Amarela, which is often described as looking like a distorted and wrinkled finger, with its indentations and slight curvature. But its main claim to fame is its light green colour which goes creamy white as it matures, before finally turning light yellow.

You will see a number of chillies called Ají or Chilli Amarela because 'amarela' is the Portuguese word for 'yellow'. They have a sweet, lemon-citrus flavour in among the heat, a sign that this is definitely a *Capsicum chinense*.

### POD DESCRIPTION

The pods start light green, become a very creamy white colour before they mature to light yellow, and are about 6cm long and 2cm wide.

### GROWING INFO

A compact plant that is a good producer. Seeds for this chilli are not widely available.

### SEED SUPPLIERS

PBPC, PSEU, RFC, UKCS

### USAGE

With its distinctive, almost white colour, this would make a very interesting chilli powder or a single-variety sauce.

# 68 Ají Pinguita de Mono

SPECIES
........................................
*C. baccatum*

SCOVILLE
RATING
........................
70,000–80,000
SHU

I have included this chilli just because I love the name. I am told the name translates from Portuguese as 'little monkey's penis' or 'little monkey's dick'.

A native of the jungles of Peru, one can find them described as both *Capsicum baccatum* and *C. annuum* but I suspect it is a case of different chillies that look similar sharing the same name. Once removed from the plant, chillies are very hard to categorically identify. Generally, the majority of chillies called Ají are *C. baccatum* (meaning 'berry-like') and they have a slightly sweeter taste, but the *C. annuum* (misleadingly, meaning 'annual') has such a variety of pod shapes it is easily misidentified without seeing the original plant and flowers.

POD DESCRIPTION

The pods only grow to about 4cm long and 1.5cm wide and they gently taper to a rounded tip. The pods ripen from green to red.

GROWING INFO

A small plant, growing to approximately 50cm high, it likes full sun and a warm environment. In cool-temperate climates, move it indoors well before any frost if you want to overwinter it.

SEED SUPPLIERS

HS, SLP

AKA

Mono Pinguita, Pipi Mono.

# 69 Apache F1

**SPECIES**

*C. annuum*

**POD DESCRIPTION**

The wide, conical pods
3cm long and 1.5cm wide
and ripen from light
green to bright red.

**GROWING INFO**

This is a great novice
plant which can be
grown in large pots and
does not need constant
maintenance. You can
grow them in a pot on
the windowsill or in a
conservatory in cool-
temperate climates.

**SEED SUPPLIERS**

BPC, NN, SDCF, SLP, SS

This is a beautiful, small, compact chilli plant
which grows to just 35–45cm high and produces
loads of small, wide, conical pods that ripen from
light green to bright red. Pick them as they ripen
and this will keep the plant productive.

Unlike many other smaller ornamental chilli
plants, this one is not only hot but also tastes
just as you expect a chilli to taste, with no bitter
aftertaste – just sweet, hot and savoury.

The little pods are packed with seeds, but
unfortunately, as an F1 variety (see page 9), seed
saving will not get you the same variety if you
grow them on the next year.

These have won a Royal Horticultural Society
Award of Garden Merit (AGM) in the UK,
which recognizes its excellence for ordinary use,
availability and stability. Seeds are available
almost everywhere.

**SCOVILLE
RATING**

70,000–80,000
SHU

# 70

# Turtle Claw & Submarine

SPECIES

*C. chinense*

POD DESCRIPTION

Turtle Claw: small, knobbly, elongated pods, 3–4cm × 1cm that ripen to a very pale yellow. Submarine: pods are 4cm long and 1.2cm wide and ripen to bright yellow.

GROWING INFO

Both the Turtle Claw and the Submarine grow well in cool-temperate climates in a greenhouse or polytunnel. They are both very productive and are also happy in a large pot.

SEED SUPPLIERS

PSEU, SLP, SSS

The Turtle Claw chilli, which is a most unusual-looking Habanero variety, produces small, elongated pods that ripen from lime-green to a pale, almost white, yellow colour.

The flavour is definitely a Habanero but with a more pronounced lemony citrus combination, great for making a fruity hot sauce.

It is known in some regions as the Aribibi Gusano ('gusano' is Spanish for 'worm'), but the name I like best is Caterpillar Pepper. If you look at a bunch of pods together they genuinely look like caterpillars or grubs. This is not the easiest of seeds to germinate, but well worth the attempt.

The Submarine is a new variety from Sea Spring Seeds (see page 223) that was developed from the Turtle Claw in an attempt to make it a more commercial success. It is a larger plant with a higher yield and the pods are more substantial, with a more intense flavour and a small bump in heat to 135,000 SHU. Most significantly, the pods ripen to a pleasing bright lemon-yellow.

If you grow either of these varieties you will not be disappointed. There is always someone working on a chilli or pepper variety to try to improve it and the Submarine is one example of this ongoing development.

SCOVILLE RATING

70,000–135,000 SHU

# 71 Thai Dragon

SPECIES

*C. annuum*

POD DESCRIPTION

This is a great early variety which can produce hundreds of 5–8-cm long, slender pods per plant. The pods start dark green and mature to a bright red.

GROWING INFO

Another must-grow chilli, always a good producer of very usable pods, successful in a grow-bag, large pot or in the ground. It likes the sun, and is excellent in the greenhouse in cool-temperate climates. Highly recommended for the novice grower.

SEED SUPPLIERS

CB, CH, NN, PSEU, SLP, TF, TWF

USAGE

Being thin skinned, pods are ideal for drying and making flakes or powder.

This is one of the first chillies I ever grew, with the Super Chile (see page 134), and both of these will always be found on my growing list. In 2006, the Royal Horticultural Society in the UK grew these as part of a trial of 51 chilli pepper varieties. Eighteen of the submitted varieties, including my favourites – the Thai Dragon and the Super Chile – received a much coveted Royal Horticultural Society Award of Garden Merit (AGM).

I grow these to make my own hot version of Thai sweet chilli sauce, using garlic, sugar, sherry vinegar and tomato ketchup. I'd never go back to the sugary bottled stuff again.

SCOVILLE RATING

75,000–100,000 SHU

# 72 Prairie Fire

**SPECIES**

*C. annuum*

**POD DESCRIPTION**

Upright pods that are 1.5cm long and 5mm in diameter. They start pale yellow, turning orange and then finally red.

**GROWING INFO**

An ideal pot plant as it is small and compact. They are easy to grow and even when fully loaded with pods will not need support.

**SEED SUPPLIERS**

NN, PSEU, SDCF, SLP, SSS, TCPC, TWF, VNG

**USAGE**

An excellent and colourful ornamental house plant.

Prairie Fire has a few meanings to chilli-heads. It is not only a variety of chilli, but also the name given to a drink laced with hot sauce. This drink started as the forfeit for losing a bet, the original being a whisky with Tabasco sauce added, but over the years other sauces and alcoholic drinks have been substituted, with the concoction sometimes even being set on fire before being downed in one.

The Prairie Fire chilli is a low-growing, multi-branching variety that produces hundreds of small, upright pods that sit above the foliage.

Its low stature makes this variety perfect as a house pot plant, with the upright nature of the colourful pods making it very attractive. As house plants, if kept away from cold conditions, they can last for many years, producing more pods each year.

Described as an ornamental, the pods of this chilli are not the most tasty, but can be added to dishes to give a quick buzz of heat. Being small and thin fleshed, they dry well and you will see dried pods like these for sale in grinders, so this could be a DIY source of replacement pods.

SCOVILLE RATING

80,000–100,000 SHU

# 73 Siling Labuyo

SPECIES

*C. frutescens*

POD DESCRIPTION

The pods stand erect from the stems, growing to 2.5–4cm long and 7.5mm wide. Most local varieties ripen from green to red, but there are also varieties that ripen to yellow and purple.

GROWING INFO

Likes it warm and humid, in cool-temperate climates this is a greenhouse- or polytunnel-only variety.

SEED SUPPLIERS

BPC, TWF

AKA

Chileng Bundok, Katumbal, Kitikot, Pasitis, Pasite, Rimorimo, Siling Bundok, Siling Kolikot, Siling Palay, Silit-diablo.

This is a small, Tabasco-type chilli (see page 126) from the Philippines. Translated from Tagalog, one of the languages of the Philippines, 'labuyo' is 'wild' and 'siling' is 'chilli', so in English this means 'wild chilli'. A Philippine chocolate company makes a dark chocolate flavoured with Siling Labuyo. This is on my must-try list when I can get hold of a bar.

This chilli has been added to the Slow Food Foundation Ark of Taste (see page 9) as it is being overshadowed by imported Bird's Eye chillies (see page 166), which are larger, milder and, unfortunately, cheaper.

This chilli makes an excellent sweet chilli sauce and it takes only a few minutes. Put 125ml water, 250g granulated sugar and 175ml white wine vinegar in a saucepan and bring to the boil, then simmer to reduce to a syrup (ten minutes should do). Meanwhile, finely chop 40–50 Siling Labuyo chillies, add to the syrup and continue to simmer while stirring for 2–3 minutes. Pour into a sterilized jar and store in the refrigerator once cooled, or use it straight away (I normally cannot resist and have to make twice as much as I need).

SCOVILLE RATING

80,000–100,000 SHU

# 74 Wiri Wiri

SPECIES

*C.frutescens,*
*C.chinense*

POD DESCRIPTION

The pod size does vary,
but typically it is 1–1.5cm
in diameter and matures
from light green to red.

GROWING INFO

Will grow to 50cm
tall, produces lots of
small pods and likes
warm, consistent
temperatures. A
definite greenhouse- or
polytunnel-variety in
cool-temperate climates.

SEED SUPPLIERS

SSS

USAGE

Used to make pepper
sauce in their native
Guyana.

On asking where Guyana is, I was given a lot of strange answers, but it is on the northwest side of South America just above Brazil with Suriname on its right and Venezuela on the left. Eighty per cent of the country is still untouched Amazon forest and it is from here that the Wiri Wiri chilli originates.

The compact Wiri Wiri plant produces a small, round, cherry-shaped pod.

I have seen it described as both *Capsicum frutescens* and *C. chinense* and both statements are to some degree true. Both these species probably shared the same common ancestors and some people think that these two species should be combined.

In their native Guyana, the most popular use for these pods is to make a pepper sauce. Large numbers of them are chopped finely and added to mango flesh, white vinegar, lots of garlic and salt, then blended together. The salt and the vinegar preserve them by increasing the acidity, but, as the sauce is not cooked, make it in small batches, as needed, as it will not keep.

SCOVILLE
RATING

80,000–150,000
SHU

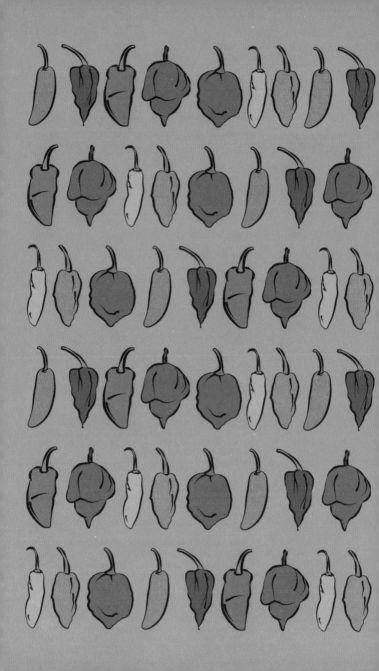

# Hot

Goronog

Bird's Eye

Prik Kee Nu

Bahamian Goat

Datil

Fatalii

Madame Jeanette

Orange Habanero

Scotch Bonnet

Pimenta de Neyde

Peruvian White Habanero

Devil's Tongue Yellow & Red

Red Savina Habanero

Pink Tiger

# 75 Goronong

**SPECIES**

*C.chinense*

**POD DESCRIPTION**

The smooth-skinned pods are 6–8cm and start a light green, turning to a light yellow and finally to a deep yellow-orange. They can grow into very unusual, twisted shapes.

This is a Malaysian variety of Habanero, and while it has a smooth skin it can produce some of the most twisted shaped pods that I have seen, with deep contours and crevices. Milder than most of the other Habaneros listed in this book, with the exception of the Apricot (500–700 SHU) and Zavory (0 SHU), at around 100,000 SHU this is much hotter than the Jalapeño that most people know which ranges from just 2,500 to 10,000 SHU.

What makes this a recommended variety is the exceptionally tasty, sweet and fruity citrus flavour, and the abundance of pods this relatively easy-to-grow plant can produce. The 6–8cm long pods start a light green and then turn a light yellow, but as they mature they take on a much deeper yellow-orange hue.

You will see them listed in seed catalogues as the Malaysian Goronong or Cili Goronong, Cili being the Malaysian for chilli, but I have also found them called Caronong or Coronong.

Use these to make a fresh salsa, with a few yellow tomatoes, finely chopped sweet onions and some coriander – hot but very yummy.

**GROWING INFO**

**Will grow to 60cm wide and 60cm high and grows well in a large container. It likes a sunny position but is best grown in a poly-tunnel or greenhouse in cooler climates.**

**SEED SUPPLIERS**

**CCN, SLP, TWF, UKCS**

**AKA**

**Malaysian Goronong, Cili Goronong**

SCOVILLE RATING

100,000–150,000 SHU

# 76 Bird's Eye

SPECIES

*C. annuum*

SCOVILLE
RATING

100,000–200,000
SHU

The Bird's Eye chilli is not a single variety, but it is a very popular name for a style of chilli found commonly all over Africa and Asia.

The common factors in the Bird's Eye chillies seem to be the small, compact size and the colour. Varieties range from 1–3cm in length and 5mm–1cm in width, tapering to a point. All of them are thin skinned and mature from green to red. This description could cover hundreds of varieties and, so it seems, it does.

There is no register for chilli names, so a good name seems to stick and may get used again and again. I have seen them listed as *Capsicum annuum*, *C. frutescens* and even as *C. chinense* (see page 6).

Of the many chillies listed as Bird's Eye, I would look for the African Bird's Eye chilli, often just called Piri Piri or Pili Pili, which in Swahili translates to 'pepper pepper'.

The African Bird's Eye chilli has a small pod, no bigger than 2cm long and 1cm wide. The pods point skyward from this bushy plant, which can grow to over 1m high, but seems to be happy confined in pots if needed.

So if a recipe calls for Bird's Eye peppers, just pick one that is small and fiery, and you won't go too far wrong.

## POD DESCRIPTION

The pods are 1–3cm long and 5mm–1cm wide, tapering to a point. They mature from green to red.

## GROWING INFO

A simple variety to grow. They expect a warm sunny environment and are often grown in conservatories.

## SEED SUPPLIERS

Almost every supplier has some kind of chilli that they call a Bird's Eye so take your pick.

## AKA

African Bird's Eye, African Devil, Bird's, Boonie Pepper, Cabe Rawit (Indonesian), Cengek (Sudanese), Cengis (Banyumasan), Cili Padi (Malay), Congo Chilli, Kanthari Mulagu (Malayalam), Kochchi (Sinhalese), Ladâ, Lombok Rawit (Javanese), Mombassa Chilli, Pequin Chilli, Phrik Khi Nu (Thai), Piri Piri, Siling Labuyo (Tagalog/Filipino), Thai Dragon, Thai Hot, Uganda Chilli, Zanzibar Chilli.

# 77

## Prik Kee Nu

SPECIES

*C. frutescens*

POD DESCRIPTION

Small pods, 2–3cm long.

GROWING INFO

Likes it hot and humid and will produce a large plant covered in pods if you can get the conditions right. It does not like big changes in temperature.

SEED SUPPLIERS

CB, CSB, HS, PBPC, PSEU, SLP

This tiny, fiery chilli comes from Thailand and is also found in Indonesian and Malaysian cuisine. It is much shorter and a lot hotter that the better-known Thai Hot chilli or Bird's Eye (see page 166). The name translates as 'mouse shit chilli' (prik = chilli, kee = shit and nu = mouse). Don't be put off by the name; it best describes the size and shape of the chillies, not the taste.

SCOVILLE
RATING
100,000–250,000
SHU

When grown in a large pot, it will reach 50–60cm high and produce a mass of small pods. This is not the easiest chilli to grow in cooler climates unless you have a polytunnel as its native climate is humid and warm. A good alternative can be the Rooster Spur, a smaller, more manageable plant.

Prik Kee Nu are the small, whole pods you find in tom yum soup and they are also used to make nam phrik sauce (which means 'fluid chilli'). This is very simple to make and is used liberally as a condiment with rice and noodles.

To make a simple nam phrik sauce, finely slice 10 Prik Kee Nu chillies, peel and crush 2–3 garlic cloves, and place in a bowl. Add 100ml Thai fish sauce, 120ml lime juice, 2 teaspoons dark brown sugar and mix well. Store in an airtight container overnight in the refrigerator before use. Remember, in Thailand this would all be done with great skill in a pestle and mortar.

# 78 Bahamian Goat

SPECIES

*C. chinense*

POD DESCRIPTION

These mature to a pale orange peach colour and are 3–4cm wide and 4–5cm long. Some will produce a small scorpion-style tail from the base.

GROWING INFO

Not one of the easiest chillies to germinate, it needs a temperature of 21–23°C and some patience, but once it gets going it will produce a lot of pods, though these can be slow to finally ripen.

SEED SUPPLIERS

BPC, CH, NN, PZW, SLP, SS, UKCS

Bahamian Goat originates from the Bahamas and looks similar in shape to a Scotch Bonnet (see page 180). The pods mature to a pale orange-peach colour. These are very similar to the Habanero and can take a long time to germinate, but it's worth it as the plants grow to about 1m tall and, in ideal conditions, can produce a heavy crop.

The Bahamas Ministry of Agriculture, Marine Resources and Local Government has recognized the Bahamian Goat pepper, along with the other local speciality, the Finger pepper, as of special interest and it has started a process of protection and improvement to increase the hardiness and yield of the crop through careful seed selection. Seeds are also protected in a seed bank as a back-up in case of natural disasters.

SCOVILLE RATING

100,000–300,000 SHU

# Datil

**SPECIES**

*C. chinense*

**POD DESCRIPTION**

Yellow-orange pods are up to 6cm long and 2.5cm wide.

**GROWING INFO**

Some of these plant can last for decades in Florida and they are prolific producers of pods. They like warm conditions and in cool-temperate climates this is a polytunnel or greenhouse plant. The seeds can be slow to germinate.

**SEED SUPPLIERS**

CH, CT, NMSU, NN, UKCS

**SCOVILLE RATING**

100,000–300,000 SHU

It is the regional specialities that make chillies so interesting and unique heritage chillies are now grown around the world. The Datil is one example and has its regional home in St Augustine, Florida, USA.

The Minorcan community there (originally from the Spanish Balearic Islands) has taken this chilli and made it their own. As far as I know, the Datil pepper was not historically grown on the Balearic Islands, so this chilli did not do a round trip to Florida via early Spanish explorers.

With its similar heat to the Orange Habanero (see page 178) to which it is probably closely related, the yellow-orange Datil pods grow to 6cm long and 2.5cm wide.

To survive for hundreds of years, a variety needs a few heroes who grow the plants and collect seeds and create the recipes that use them. In this case, it seems that the dish was the Minorcan Clam Chowder, a fiery, tomato-based chowder that is hugely popular in the St Augustine area. Recently, the First Coast Technical College in St Augustine has been growing and selling Datil seeds. In 2007, the Datil Pepper Festival started, with local professional chefs showing off their skills with the Datil chilli to win the People's Choice Award.

Whatever its origins, this pepper is moving from a plant grown and known only in Florida to one with a worldwide audience. Seeds are now starting to appear in the online seed catalogues. In 2008, it was included in the Slow Food Foundation Ark of Taste (see page 9), which can only help increase its visibility.

# 80 Fatalii

SPECIES
...........................................
*C. chinense*

SCOVILLE
RATING
.........................................
100,000–300,000
SHU

A close relation of the Red Savina Habanero (see page 188) and the Scotch Bonnet chillies (see page 180), the Fatalii comes from Central Africa.

Ideal for the first-time grower, the plants grow to around 60cm tall or more and are easy to grow in full sun. Perhaps I use the term 'citrus' too often to describe chillies and, maybe it is the bright yellow colour of this one that makes me think so, but it has a definite lemon-lime hint to it.

A red variety of Fatalii is also available. This is a natural mutation and some plants will produce both yellow and red peppers at the same time.

## POD DESCRIPTION

**The pods start green and ripen to a lemon-yellow colour and can grow to 6cm long and 3cm wide, tapering to a point.**

## GROWING INFO

**This is a sun lover. In cool-temperate climates, a bright, sunny place in a greenhouse or polytunnel is best. Lots of good-quality seeds are available, giving high germination rates.**

## SEED SUPPLIERS

**BPC, BS, CF, CH, CSB, NN, PBPC, SDCF, SLP, SS, SSS, UKCS**

## USAGE

**A number of excellent sauces make use of this chilli.**

# 81

# Madame Jeanette

SPECIES

*C. chinense*

SCOVILLE
RATING

100,000–350,000
SHU

A close relation to the Orange Habanero (see page 178) and the Red Savina Habanero (see page 188), the Madame Jeanette may get its name from a professional lady of dubious virtue from Paramaribo, the capital city of Suriname, though others have given her Brazilian nationality. Whatever the truth or lack of it, this chilli still packs a punch at up to 350,000 Scoville units.

Suriname, officially called the Republic of Suriname, is on the northeastern coast of South America. It was colonized by the Dutch who governed until 1975, when it became an independent country.

The Suriname Red is also often called the Madame Jeanette, but the pods of the Suriname Red pods turn red when fully ripe, rather than yellow/orange.

### POD DESCRIPTION

The pods are 5–7cm long and 3–4cm wide. They start light green and turn a golden-yellow to orange colour. They look a little more tortured than the Habanero with a generally more wrinkled appearance.

### GROWING INFO

The plants grow to well over 1m high in the right warm and sunny conditions. Seeds are becoming available for the yellow and red variants, but they are still not common. If you have grown Habaneros successfully, then why not give these a try?

### SEED SUPPLIERS

SLP

### AKA

Suriname Yellow.

# 82 Orange Habanero

SPECIES

*C. chinense*

SCOVILLE
RATING

100,000–350,000
SHU

Anyone who likes heat will know the Orange Habanero. As a Habanero, it is one of the most common and best known. It is also one of the hotter varieties, and has been around for a very long time, pretty much becoming the standard for Habaneros.

When I started growing chillies, the Red and Orange Habanero were considered some of the hardest to grow, but as the enthusiasm of the amateur growers for more interesting varieties and the quality of seeds improved, these are now seen as commonplace.

If you are going to grow just one type of Habanero, make Orange Habanero the one. Its balance of flavour, heat and the number of pods produced will pay back your efforts in trumps.

## POD DESCRIPTION

The lantern-shaped pods start dark green and mature to orange, growing to 2–3cm wide and 4cm long. Pick the pods as soon as they are ripe to spur the plant on to producing more.

## GROWING INFO

A favourite to grow and very popular, there are lots of good-quality seeds available with high germination rates. The plants are very adaptable and, when grown in small pots the plants will be small, while in bigger pots they will be proportionally bigger. In all cases, the variety is very productive.

## SEED SUPPLIERS

BPC, BS, CF, CH, CSB, HS, LS, MWCH, NMSU, NN, PBPC, PN, PSEU, PZW, RFC, SDCF, SLP, SS, SSS, TF, TWF, UKCS

## USAGE

There is a rich supply of recipes from Mexico and the Caribbean and Orange Habanero also makes a great chutney.

# 83 Scotch Bonnet

SPECIES

*C. chinense*

SCOVILLE
RATING

100,000–350,000
SHU

These peppers are said to get their name from the tam o'shanter, or Scottish bonnet, historically worn by Scottish men. This chilli originated in the Caribbean and it gives jerk dishes their unique heat and flavour. Its connection to jerk cuisine has made this pepper one of the first to be well known around the world – a Jamaican goat curry without Scotch Bonnet is just unthinkable.

Scotch Bonnet is closely related to other Habanero varieties, like the Red Savina Habanero (see page 188), and has similar heat levels but a quite different flavour. Over the past few years, an ever-growing number of varieties has been developed and mutated by growers.

West Indian Scotch Bonnet pepper sauce is one of the simplest sauces to make and each West Indian family probably has its own variation on the recipe. The simplest, and the one I use, has just Scotch Bonnet peppers, salt and distilled white vinegar blended together and bottled. Do not add too much salt to start. You are trying to make a thin sauce.

## POD DESCRIPTION

Traditional-variety pods grow to 3–4cm long and 2–3cm wide, ripening from green to either red or yellow, but there are brown and even pink versions now too.

## GROWING INFO

Like the Jalapeño (see page 60) and Serrano (see page 88), this is one of the seeds that most suppliers seem to stock. It used to be considered at the difficult end of the growing spectrum, but the increasing quality of the seeds and better knowledge of growing conditions now make this moderately difficult to grow.

## SEED SUPPLIERS

BCS, BPC, BS, CB, CF, CH, CSB, HS, LS, MWCH, NN, PBPC, PJ, PSEU, PZW, RFC, SDCF, SLP, SS, TWF, UKCS

## AKA

Boabs Bonnet, Bonney Pepper, Caribbean Red Pepper, Scotty Bon.

# 84 Pimenta de Neyde

SPECIES

*C. annuum*
*C. chinense*

SCOVILLE
RATING

150,000–250,000
SHU

Supposedly named after Neyde Hidalgo, the lady who discovered it growing in her garden in Brazil, the Pimenta de Neyde produces dark purple pods that become a brighter, more luminescent purple as it matures.

The stems and leaves on the plant are also dark purple like the pods. It has long stems and produces a small tree-shaped plant. It is thought to be a cross between a *Capsicum chinense* and a *C. annuum*, but without some genetic work this is just pure speculation.

Seeds are available via specialist suppliers, and, if you have the space, Pimenta de Neyde would be an interesting one to grow and from which to produce further crosses.

## POD DESCRIPTION

The pods grow to 6–8cm long and taper out to 2cm wide and then back to a rounded tip. Cut open the pods and the inside of the thick flesh, placenta and veins seems almost white in comparison to the skin.

## GROWING INFO

This grows well, and can reach over 80cm tall.

## SEED SUPPLIERS

BPC, HS, LS, NN, PSEU, RFC, SLP, TCPC, TWF

# 85

# Peruvian White Habanero

SPECIES

*C. chinense*

POD DESCRIPTION

The pods start lime-green and turn a creamy white. Each plant can produce an abundance of these little 3–5-cm elongated, white pods.

GROWING INFO

You will need to be prepared for a few losses to grow this one as it likes optimal growing conditions with little variation in warmth.

SEED SUPPLIERS

BPC, BS, CB, CCN, CF, CH, CSB, HS, LS, MWCH, PN, PSEU, RFC, SS, TCPC, TF, TWF

AKA

Yucatán White Habanero.

Probably from Peru, but also known as the Yucatán White Habanero, so may originate in Mexico, these little, white chilli pods pack a hefty punch.

These bullet-shaped pods have been described as 'jelly-bean like' by Neil Smith from The Hippy Seed Company (see page 222), and that description could not be more apt.

They are very similar to the slightly smaller Habanero White Bullet® from the Redwood City Seed Company. In the past ten years, we have seen a profusion of Habanero varieties coming on to the market, providing a range of colours including red, orange, yellow, brown, white, purple and even black.

Peruvian White Habaneros are notoriously hard to grow, as the plant is very susceptible to almost any change from the optimal growing conditions, that is if you can get a reliable source of seeds that germinate.

They are most often grown for their novelty value than for their flavour, which is slightly citrus. This chilli would be good for adding some hidden heat to a white sauce.

SCOVILLE RATING

150,000–300,000 SHU

# 86

# Devil's Tongue Yellow & Red

SPECIES

*C. chinense*

POD DESCRIPTION

**Devil's Tongue Yellow: wedge-shaped pods, 4–7cm long and 2–4cm wide. Devil's Tongue Red: larger and bright red.**

GROWING INFO

**Another chilli where the germination can be a bit slow; this is a recurring theme with the hotter varieties.**

SEED SUPPLIERS

**BPC, BS, CH, CSB, HS, NN, RFC, SLP, UKCS**

An Amish farmer in Pennsylvania, USA, is believed to have originated the Devil's Tongue Yellow. At the right angle pods can look like a wrinkled tongue. It has a very similar flavour and heat level to an Orange Habanero (see page 178), but has a more wedge-shaped and wrinkled pod. The pods are thin fleshed and grow to 4–7cm long, depending on how the tongue shape develops, and 2–4cm wide.

The Devil's Tongue Red is said to have been developed from the Devil's Tongue Yellow, but this is pure conjecture, based on the name and shape. It is larger and hotter, with a more sweet, fruity flavour than the yellow variety. With its bright red colour, it can look even more like a tongue shape.

Like a lot of these unusual variations, try to buy seeds from a reliable source that has a history of supplying quality seeds. As most people have never seen these varieties, it is easy to be sold the cheaper and much more common Yellow or Red Habanero seeds. A highly recommended source of these seeds is Jim Duffy of Refining Fire Chiles (see page 223), who grows and sells both the yellow and red varieties.

SCOVILLE RATING

250,000–500,000 SHU

# 87

# Red Savina Habanero

**SPECIES**

*C. chinense*

**POD DESCRIPTION**

The pods are 2–6cm long and 2.5–4cm wide.

**GROWING INFO**

These used to be considered hard to germinate but, compared to some of the super hots, they are a breeze. They do like warm conditions, but not always direct sunlight. The plants grow to 1m tall and can produce 50 pods in a good season.

**SEED SUPPLIERS**

BPC, BS, CF, CH, CSB, HS, LS, MWCH, NN, PBPC, PJ, PSEU, PZW, RFC, SLP, SS, TF, UKCS

When I first got involved in chillies many years ago, this was the most feared chilli. It rated at a seemingly mind-boggling. 577,000 SHU and was held in even greater reverence than the Bhut Jolokia (see page 200) and the rest of the million-plus club are today. I still have a bottle of pure Red Savina mash, the processed pulped flesh of the chilli, which I kept as a collector's item. Today, I can buy supposedly far hotter chillies in my local supermarket.

The Red Savina held the official Guinness World Record from 1994 to 2007. Originally found growing in a field of Orange Habaneros (see page 178), Frank Garcia of GNS Spices in Walnut, California harvested the red pods, dehydrated them and saved the seeds. He selectively bred them to produce larger, heavier, hotter pods, which achieved the then record-breaking 577,000 SHU in 1994.

The Orange Habanero can get as hot as 350,000 SHU so, at the time, a jump to 577,000 SHU was a big increase. In some recent tests, Sea Spring Seeds, the developer of the Dorset Naga (see page 209), grew as many super hots as they could obtain and had them tested at the end of the season. Not one of the chillies passed 400,000 SHU, and this shows just how variable chillies can be and also the quality of the stabilization of some of the varieties. You may think you are eating a 1.5-million-SHU chilli, but it could be that the old Red Savina Habanero is hotter and more consistent.

**SCOVILLE RATING**

350,000–577,000 SHU

# 88

# Pink Tiger

SPECIES
...............................................

*C.chinense*

POD DESCRIPTION
...............................................

This is an unstable
variety and pods vary
hugely in size, shape
and colour.

The Pink Tiger is a very interesting hybrid of the Bhut Jolokia (AKA the Ghost chilli) and the Pimenta da Neyde. As far as my research has found it is a very unstable hybrid, with plants producing many different shaped pods.

I believe the original idea of its producer was to produce a hybrid of the Bhut Jolokia and the Pimenta da Neyde to produce a purple Bhut Jolokia. In 2009 Paolo Fisicaro produced a hybrid of these two that was named the Elisa Pimenta AISPES (AISPES is an Italian non-profit association that works with professional and novice breeders to collect, preserve and spread the Solanaceae family genus, which is included in some chillies, tomatoes and other flowering plants). Work is still ongoing to make this a stable variety.

I suspect the Pink Tiger has come out of the AISPES breeding programme. Though it is not a purple Bhut Jolokia, it can produce beautifully variegated pods that grow to 5–8cm long. The pods start green and quickly turn purple with cream or peach stripes or spots. I'm told they are capable of turning red if left for long enough.

The taste of this chilli is strongly reminiscent of the Bhut Jolokia, but without the initial searing heat. The only samples I have tried have been much milder than expected but I have read reports rating them with similar heat levels to the Bhut Jolokia. This is more likely due to the great variability of this variety rather than the toughness of my palate.

GROWING INFO

Unstable varieties are always hard to grow since you never quite know what you are going to get. This should grow to between 60–80cm high and will need a warm and sunny position. It is best in a poly-tunnel or greenhouse in cooler climates.

SEED SUPPLIERS

SLP, TCPC, UKCS

SCOVILLE RATING

400,000–500,000 SHU (estimated)

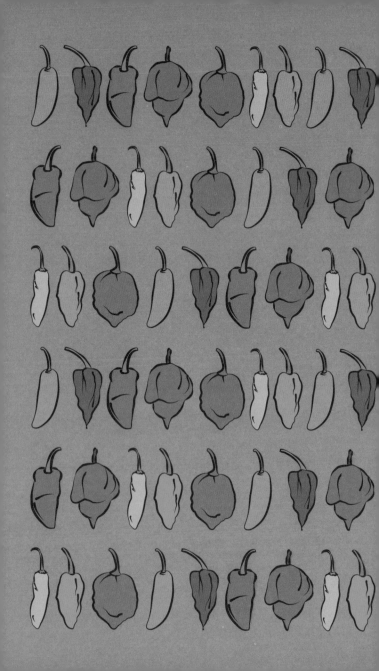

# Very Hot

Nagabon Jolokia

Bubblegum 7 & Borg 9

7 Pot

Bhut Jolokia

Habalokia

Infinity

Douglah, Chocolate 7 Pot

Dorset Naga

# 89 Nagabon Jolokia

**SPECIES**

*C. chinense*

**POD DESCRIPTION**

Pods grow to 5–8cm long and 2–3cm wide.

**GROWING INFO**

For such a hot pepper, this needs little maintenance. It germinates well and would be a good choice for a novice to grow.

**SEED SUPPLIERS**

CH, CSB, HS, SLP

A few years ago, The Hippy Seed Company in New South Wales, Australia (see page 222), supplied The Chilli Factory (see page 222) with some Bih Jolokia seeds. Out of the 500 plants they grew, one was a little different, looking a little more like a Scotch Bonnet (see page 180). This was nicknamed the 'NagaBon' (a Naga Bhut Jolokia that looks like a Scotch Bonnet) and The Hippy Seed Company collected some of the seeds and started the process of stabilizing the variety.

Now, Nagabon seeds are available from The Hippy Seed Company and a few other specialists. The pods are larger than average for a Naga cross, growing to 5–8cm long and 2–3cm wide, and some weigh over 10g. The plant has the look of a Naga and grows to over 1m high, but the pods are more Scotch Bonnet-like.

The true ancestry of this chilli may never be known, but I love the name and it will forever be linked to the Scotch Bonnet.

SCOVILLE RATING

700,000–800,000 SHU

# 90

# Bubblegum 7 & Borg 9

SPECIES

*C. chinense*

**SCOVILLE RATING**

250,000–1,000,000
(estimated, as not
officially tested)

These two chillies are included together as they both come from chilli enthusiast Jon Harper. He is not a professional grower nor, as far as I know, a geneticist, but he has produced a couple of chillies that have been talked about enthusiastically on the online forums.

The first is the Bubblegum 7, which came from seeds saved from a Moruga Scorpion. The pods produced were larger than expected, the calyx (the base of the flower, that then forms the top of the chilli where the stem connects) also produced a surprise. Normally green, this one turned red as the chilli ripened. Jon named this one after Bubblicious Bubblegum, which is the taste it reminded him of. When my colleague Chris tried it, bubblegum was the last thing on his mind, as the burn tried to rip out his throat.

The Borg 9 got its name when Jon read that Ernest Borgnine had died, and it seems an apt tribute. It has come from a cross of the Bubblegum 7 and the Naglah, itself a cross of the Naga Bhut Jolokia and the Douglah (see page 206). The Naglah was named by the late Chilli Pepper Pete, else we may have been seeing the Douglabhut, and I don't think anyone wanted that to see the light of day.

You may find some online seed companies selling Jon's creations, but they may not be very stable varieties as Jon is still working on these. Chillies are fun to play with as they cross easily, but producing stable varieties can take years, and in many cases this inbuilt instability is what produces the most interesting traits.

## POD DESCRIPTION

These can look very similar but, with the Bubblegum 7, the red colour can extend into the larger-than-normal, red cap and stem. Both varieties have a heavily textured and wrinkled skin.

## GROWING INFO

These varieties are for the enthusiast known for being unstable varieties, you cannot be sure what you will get and germination rates can also be very low.

## SEED SUPPLIERS

BPC, CF, NN, SLP, UKCS

# 91 7 Pot

SPECIES

*C. chinense*

SCOVILLE
RATING

700,000–1,200,000
SHU

Originating from Trinidad, the 7 Pot was almost unknown to the world of chilli-heads until just a few years ago. The Caribbean Agricultural Research and Development Institute lists this chilli as the 7 Pod, but it has become better known to the chilli community as the 7 Pot, with the accompanying old wives' tale that it gets this name from its ability to flavour seven pots of stew.

Even in the few years since 7 Pot has emerged, there are already many variations on the theme coming forward. In online seed catalogues, you will find 7 Pot Orange, 7 Pot Burgundy, 7 Pot Yellow, 7 Pot Chaguanas Red (Chaguanas is a town in Trinidad around which this chilli was said to originate), Chocolate 7 Pot (see page 206), 7 Pot Jonah, to name but a few. These varieties may be stable, but experience tells me that it takes many years to get a new variety fully stable.

Each colour variation is caused by cross-pollination with another variety at some point and these variations may be stable but only time will tell. Variations occur naturally as plants are cross-pollinated by insects, which is the way we get such a diverse variety of species.

It is likely all the super hot chillies coming from Trinidad share a common ancestry. Neil Smith at The Hippy Seed Company (see page 222) has been working on a cross between a Yellow Scotch Bonnet and the 7 Pot and has produced what he is calling the NeBru 7 Pot, which has resulted in a pod that matures to yellow. If you hunt around, you will find many other experimental varieties.

## POD DESCRIPTION

Similar in shape to a Red Savina Habanero (see page 188) but a little shorter and wider, but the pod shape can vary with the end being inverted or pointed, some even have a small scorpion tail. In fact, overall these chillies vary considerably: some are almost smooth skinned while others have the pimpled skin found on some of the other super hot chillies, with a number of ribs and bulbous segments.

## GROWING INFO

Can be hard to germinate, so not recommended for novice growers.

## SEED SUPPLIERS

BPC, BS, CF, CH, HS, LS, NN, PBPC, SLP, SS, UKCS

## AKA

7 Pod.

# 92 Bhut Jolokia

SPECIES
..............................................
*C. chinense*

SCOVILLE
RATING
..............................................
750,000–1,500,000
SHU

In the year 2000, the India Ministry of Defence tested a locally grown chilli, known then as the Naga Jolokia ('Jolokia' meaning 'chilli pepper' and 'Naga' from the location of the chillies in Nagaland in the northeastern part of India) at 855,000 SHU.

Then, in 2004, Frontal Agritech, an Indian commercial agricultural company, tested the then-named Bih Jolokia at 1,047,427 SHU. The world record at the time was held by the Red Savina Habanero (see page 188) at 577,000 SHU.

In 2007, researchers at New Mexico State University in the USA claimed the world record for heat at 1,001,304 SHU, for what became known as the Ghost chilli, which was grown from seeds collected in India in 2001.

Work published by New Mexico State University shows this chilli to be a naturally occurring, interspecific hybrid and, while it was mostly *Capsicum chinense*, some traits from *C. frutescens* were also identified in DNA testing.

In Germany in 2011, Guinness World Records recorded a new record for eating three Bhut Jolokia chillies in 1 minute, 11 seconds by Birgit Tack. The record for the most eaten in 2 minutes – 66g – goes to Jason McNabb from USA, on 19 June 2013.

## POD DESCRIPTION

The pods grow to 5–9cm long and 2–3cm wide, generally tapering to a point. The skin is pimpled and rough looking and the fruits can look very ridged and textured.

## GROWING INFO

This is not the simplest chilli to grow; it is slow to germinate and needs germination temperatures of 24–28°C. In cool-temperate climates it needs to be grown in a sunny polytunnel or greenhouse. Will also be slow to ripen, but you can eat the pods at any stage.

## SEED SUPPLIERS

BPC, BS, CF, CH, CSB, HS, LS, NMSU, NN, SDCF, SLP, SS, UKCS, VNG

## AKA

Bhoot Jolokia, Bih Jolokia, Borbih Jolokia, Ghost chilli, King Cobra Chilli, Malta, Nagahari, Naga Jolokia, Naga Moresh, Naga Morich, Raja Mirchi, U-Morok.

# 93 Habalokia

SPECIES

*C. chinense*

SCOVILLE
RATING

800,000–1,000,000
SHU

This is a cross between a Habanero variety and a Bhut Jolokia (see page 200), hence the name Habalokia. As with most of these new chilli varieties, there are lots of varieties that seem to go under this name. I have seen versions called Habalokia Brown, Chocolate Habalokia, Orange Habalokia and Habalokia Red, to name but a few.

These crosses are not considered stable as yet and the plants can produce erratic-styled pods and very low germination rates, but this does not seem to limit the number of seeds that have become available on the internet.

Growing unstable varieties can be very interesting. To get a stable cross can take many years' work, with the chilli plants remaining isolated during flowering and the setting of the pods, or else they may become crossed yet again with other chillies grown nearby.

Growing these is a bit of an adventure, as you are never sure what you are going to get.

## POD DESCRIPTION

**These pods are often wrinkled and a little contorted with the pimpled skin found on some of the other super hot chillies. They can grow to 5–7cm long and 2–4cm wide at the top, tapering down to a point.**

## GROWING INFO

**One of the hardest to germinate, with many growers reporting little success, which is one of the problems with many unstable varieties.**

## SEED SUPPLIERS

**BPC, LS, UKCS**

# 94 Infinity

**POD DESCRIPTION**

These have round pods with a slight taper at the bases. The skin is generally wrinkled. Pods are 3–4cm in diameter.

**GROWING INFO**

Like most very hot chillies, these can take a while to germinate and expect warm, sunny conditions.

**SEED SUPPLIERS**

BPC, CF, CH, HS, PSEU, SLP, UKCS

**SCOVILLE RATING**

800,000–1,176,182 SHU

The Infinity chilli was discovered by Nick Woods growing in his polytunnel in Grantham, UK, among all the other super hot chillies he was growing for his business Fire Foods: 'I knew as soon as I saw it in the polytunnel. It stood out, and, when I dissected it, I could tell by the skin tissue and the seeds that it was a hot one,' said Nick, who thinks it may be an accidental cross between a Trinidad Scorpion (see page 212) and a 7 Pot (see page 198).

My colleague Tony Ainsworth (AKA Darth Naga) ate a pod during a tasting in October 2009. The effects were devastating and I believe a video of this can still be found on YouTube.

Nick Woods supplied some seeds to Simpson's Seeds (see page 223) in early 2009 and samples were sent to Warwick University, UK, for testing. The result came back at 1,067,286 SHU and later tests of the 2010 crop increased this result to 1,176,182 SHU.

In March 2010, the Infinity held the Guinness World Record with the original test result of 1,067,286 SHU. The Infinity chilli did not hold the record for long. It was surpassed in February 2011 by the Naga Viper (see page 216), but it helped to fire up the race for the record. You may be able to find seeds, but they are now becoming few and far between and, as this variety was an accidental cross, it cannot be expected to be stable.

# 95

# Douglah, Chocolate 7 Pot

SPECIES

*C. chinense*

The Trinidad Douglah has shot to fame over the past couple of years as being a real contender for the world's hottest chilli. Its chocolate-brown skin is pimpled and the almost white internal membrane seems to leak capsaicin at the slightest touch.

It seems the Douglah and the Chocolate 7 Pot could be the same beast. Recent tests showed the Chocolate 7 Pot had a peak of 1,853,936 SHU, with an average of 1,169,058 SHU.

There seems to be so many variations on the Douglah/Chocolate 7 pot theme that, without some work on the genetics, we may never know the true provenance of these varieties.

The Douglah pods have a thin, wrinkly skin, starting green and maturing to a chocolate-brown. The pods are not easy to germinate and take a long time to mature. In cool-temperate climates, you will need a greenhouse or polytunnel and you should get your seedlings started early. This is not a chilli recommended for first-time growers. (Out of interest, the word 'Dougla' in the West Indies is used to describe a person who is of mixed African and East Indian descent.)

## POD DESCRIPTION

**Green, maturing to chocolate-brown, the pods grow to about 6cm long and 4–5cm wide.**

## GROWING INFO

**Hard to germinate and slow to ripen, this is a chilli for the experienced grower.**

## SEED SUPPLIERS

**BPC, BS, CF, CH, HS, LS, NN, PBPC, PZW, UKCS**

## AKA

**Brown 7 Pot.**

**SCOVILLE RATING**

**800,000–1,800,000 SHU**

# 96 Dorset Naga

SPECIES
.......................................
*C. chinense*

SCOVILLE
RATING
.......................................
876,000–970,000
SHU (although
1,598,227 SHU
in BBC tests)

Strangely originating from the Southwest coast of England, Dorset Naga must be one of the few very hot chillies that have not held the world record for heat, but it easily could have done, and could, in fact, still be the record holder today.

Developed by Joy and Michael Michaud of Sea Spring Seeds (see page 223) from the Bangladeshi Naga Morich (fairly unknown outside of the British-Bangladeshi community), the first plants grown in 2002 showed a wide diversity of plant and fruit sizes and shapes. The selection process was refined over the following years, resulting in the characteristic wedge shape and finely wrinkled skin of the Dorset Naga.

In 2005, samples tested in New Mexico and New York, USA hit 876,000 SHU and a staggering 970,000 SHU, beating the existing Guinness World Record was held by the Red Savina Habanero (see page 188) at 577,000 SHU, but the discrepancy between the two seemed so large that the Dorset Naga developers were reluctant to chase the record.

In 2006, it was included in the BBC television *Gardeners' World* chilli trial. Seeds were sent to growers around the country and the pods sent for testing at Warwick University, where the highest result given for this chilli was 1,598,227 SHU. Today, the chilli record still officially stands at 1,569,300 SHU for the Carolina Reaper chilli (see page 220), which was awarded in November 2013, some seven years later.

While never officially the world record holder, the Dorset Naga is nonetheless one of the world's hottest chillies.

## POD DESCRIPTION

These wedge-shaped pods start green and ripen to red. They can grow to 6cm long, but 4–5cm is more typical, and 3–4cm wide at the shoulders.

## GROWING INFO

Given the space, this can grow to be a massive plant. Plants with over 2,000 ripe chillies have been known. Not for the novice grower but a good introduction to very hot chillies.

## SEED SUPPLIERS

BPC, CF, CSB, HS, LS, SSS

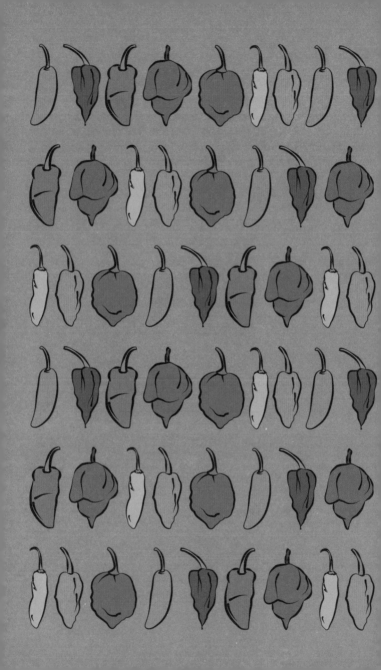

# Super Hot

**Trinidad Scorpion**

**Fatalii Gourmet Jigsaw**

**Naga Viper**

**Katie Habanero**

**Carolina Reaper (HP22B)**

# 97 Trinidad Scorpion

SPECIES

*C. chinense*

SCOVILLE
RATING

900,000–1,463,700
SHU

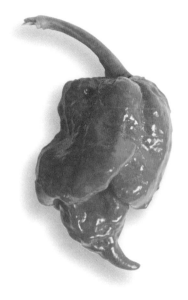

The Trinidad Scorpion gets its name from the sometime tail at the bottom of the pod. It is uncommon even in its home of Trinidad and in 2009 my friend Joseph McCullough (AKA Chilli Joe) spent his month-long holiday in Trinidad hunting for the Scorpion and its cousin the 7 Pot (see page 198). He eventually managed to track them down but fast-forwarding to 2011 the Trinidad Scorpion came to the notice of the world when a variety called Trinidad Scorpion Butch T was awarded the World Record at 1,463,700 SHU.

Grown and submitted for the record by The Chilli Factory (see page 222), the seeds for this record had been sourced from Neil Smith of The Hippy Seed Company in July 2010 (you may know Neil from his video chilli reviews on YouTube). Why is this called the Butch T? Neil called this variety the Butch T as he had obtained the seeds from Butch Taylor of Zydeco Farms, Mississippi, USA, who had been growing and developing chillies for many years.

Alex de Wit at The Chilli Factory tends his chillies with lots of love and care, giving them the best conditions for growth. Other growers use the 'treat them mean' technique, depriving them of water after the pods have formed, in the hope the plant will produce more capsaicin to protect the pods as they develop. Research is underway to see how much growing conditions affect heat, but don't expect results for a few years.

The Australian Trinidad Scorpion Butch T held the record until November 2013, when it was beaten by the Carolina Reaper (see page 220), which clocked in at 1,569,300 SHU.

## POD DESCRIPTION

The pods can grow to 4–8cm long, including the sharp pointed tail, and will ripen from green via orange to red. This can take a while in cool-temperate climates.

## GROWING INFO

Recommended for the experienced grower only, this is not the easiest chilli to grow and there is often the problem of poor germination. This chilli expects warm conditions – 20°C – before the seeds will sprout and in cool-temperate climates it definitely needs a greenhouse or polytunnel and careful attention to see any decent results. It is simpler for this and many of the other super hot chillies to order plug plants from a reputable local supplier.

## SEED SUPPLIERS

BCS, BPC, BS, CB, CCN, CF, CH, CSB, HS, LS, MWCH, NMSU, NN, PN, PSEU, PZW, RFC, SLP, TCPC, TF, TWF, UKCS, VNG

# Fatalii Gourmet Jigsaw

SPECIES

*C. chinense*

SCOVILLE
RATING

**1,200,000 SHU**
(very estimated,
no published
results)

This chilli comes from the Finnish chilli specialist Jukka Kilpinen, who runs the website Fatalii.net. His idea was to try to breed a hotter chilli using the Moruga Scorpion chilli and cross-breeding it with other super hot chillies.

Chilli breeders are well known for keeping their cross-breeds a closely guarded secret, because a successful record attempt can be worth a lot of money.

After a few years of selectively breeding among just the hottest of the chillies, the Fatalii Gourmet Jigsaw, with its bright red, shiny, contorted skin, was created. When cut open, this thin-fleshed pod reveals an oily inner lining of what I suspect is capsaicin leaking from its veins.

As far as I have been able to ascertain, there are no published test results for this chilli, so the rumour mill has been doing overtime. I have tasted both the Carolina Reaper (see page 220), which is current world record holder, and the Fatalii Gourmet Jigsaw, and both chillies completely blew me away. As I get older I don't seem to be getting any wiser – I could not tell you which was the hottest. Both caused complete havoc with my body, leaving me with little memory of any flavour before the heat hit. Others have told me that the flavour is similar to the Bhut Jolokia (see page 200), if a little sweeter and fruitier.

### POD DESCRIPTION

Like most of the super hots, this has a pimpled skin and a contorted, tapered shape. It can grow to 2–3cm wide and 4–6cm long.

### GROWING INFO

If you can get seeds then give it a go, but expect long germination times. The pods will also be slow to mature. However, if the plants can be grown successfully in the Finland climate, what have you got to lose?

### SEED SUPPLIERS

Seeds are becoming available. Try UKCS and FS for more news of this variety.

# 99 Naga Viper

SPECIES
.........................................

*C. chinense*

SCOVILLE
RATING
.........................................
1,000,000–1,382,118
SHU

This is another accidental Guinness World Record Holder at 1,382,118 SHU. It was discovered by Gerald Fowler of The Chilli Pepper Company (see page 223) and grown in Cark, Cumbria, in the UK. It is described as a three-way hybrid of a Naga Morich (see page 209), Bhut Jolokia (see page 200) and a Trinidad Scorpion (see page 212), but I was never quite sure how this was achieved.

Unfortunately, its seeds have been a little unstable and do not always produce what is expected. Work is continuing to try to produce a stable version of this variety, but this can take many generations. Some seeds are available but you may not get what you expect when they produce pods.

The Naga Viper did have a dramatic effect on Gerald Fowler's business. Within a few days of attaining the record, he had massive back orders for the sauce he had made with it and a waiting list for over 1,200 packets of seeds. A record like this brings international recognition and sales, but scaling up the success to meet demand can lead to a lot of customers being disappointed at the speed of delivery.

Growing a chilli from seedling stage to the point at which it is mature enough to provide seeds can take 90–100 days. Those seeds then need to be removed from the pod, dried and tested to make sure they germinate before packing and sending out to customers. That is no problem if you have produced a stable variety. Stabilization can take many growing seasons and careful plant selection.

### POD DESCRIPTION

They have wrinkled and contorted flesh with a lightly textured skin. They can grow to 4–6cm long and 2–3cm wide.

### GROWING INFO

Not the easiest to germinate, and probably still unstable, but can produce some stunning pods.

### SEED SUPPLIERS

BPC, CF, CH, HS, LS, PJ, PSEU, TCPC, TF, TWF, UKCS

# 100 Katie Habanero

*C. chinense*

SCOVILLE
RATING

Possibly 1,590,000
SHU

In late 2014, BBC television asked if I would appear on a programme to act as a chilli expert and to discuss this new chilli variety. I appeared with Matt Simpson of Simpson's Seeds, a well-known grower of chillies in the UK (see page 223), and Tim Woodman from Bath University. Tim had produced the provisional test results and had been working with Matt to develop a method of testing using an industrial MRI scanner (not the type the hospitals use).

Both Matt and Tim did not wish to push the results of the tests as a new record since they were tests of a very small (single-pod) sample, but the results do look promising for the future, although a larger batch would need to be randomly tested.

Matt had obtained the seeds from Nick Duran, a grower based in Somerset, England, nicknamed Naga Nick. Katie is the name of one of his daughters and there is also another Habanero called Lucy after his other daughter. This clocked in at 1,359,284 SHU.

Seeds for both of these super hot chillies are now being sold by a number of seed companies, but, with so many fakes coming to the market, make sure you get an original.

## POD DESCRIPTION

**Katie Habanero produces large pods, about 4–6cm wide, that ripen to a bright red colour. The plants grow to about 1m high.**

## GROWING INFO

**Matt Simpson at Simpson Seeds stressed his crop, removing stems and even shouting at the plants, before picking the chillies for testing. The jury is still out as to whether this worked.**

## SEED SUPPLIERS

**SS, TCPC, UKCS**

# 101 Carolina Reaper (HP22B)

SPECIES

*C. chinense*

SCOVILLE
RATING

1,569,000 average–
2,000,000+ peak

This chilli burst on the scene during 2011–12, when it appeared as HP22B. Now named the Carolina Reaper, it was awarded the Guinness World Record in November 2013.

Developed by Ed Currie, owner of Puckerbutt Pepper Company (see page 222), this chilli was worked on for over ten years. I believe the chilli was scrutinized very carefully by the Guinness World Record team after such a quick succession of records had been awarded in the previous few years. Ed tested nearly 20 kg over three years and provided an 18-page report that included data from chemistry, botany and biology over a five- to eight-year period, as well as photographic proof over nine years.

Being a brave and now stupid-feeling author, I taste tested this pod hoping to give you a full account of the flavours. I have eaten a few super hot chillies and some amazingly hot sauces over the years, but I was in over my head with this one – it nearly killed me. A few chews and the rest of my taste test was a blur followed by lots of milk and ice cream.

Ed tells me it has a sweet, fruity flavour with hints of cinnamon and chocolate, but I never got that pleasure. I have a lot of respect for the chilli-heads, including Darth Naga, Nigel Carter, Neil Smith and Chilli Dave, who record videos, make it to the end of a pod and can still talk.

News has come in from Ed about his latest creation. Currently only known as the HP56 Death Strain, this may be his next candidate for the record with latest results averaging 2,890,000 SHU.

## POD DESCRIPTION

The shape and skin of the pods need to be seen to be believed; they are contorted with pimples and bulges, before finally the stinger tail protrudes from the bottom. Pods change from light green to a crimson-red and, including the tail, they can be 7.5cm long and the same wide.

## GROWING INFO

Plants can reach over 1.5m tall so you will need lots of space, and expect a long germination period.

## SEED SUPPLIERS

BPC, CB, CCN, CF, CH, CSB, HS, MWCH, NN, PBPC, PN, PSEU, PZW, RFC, SLP, TCPC, TF, TWF, UKCS, VNG

# Seed & Plug Plant Suppliers

**BCS – Baker Creek Seeds (USA)**
*www.rareseeds.com*

**BPC – Buckeye Pepper Company (USA)**
*www.buckeyepepper.com*

**BS – Bountiful Seeds (France)**
*www.bountifulseeds.com*

**CB – Chillibird (Australia)**
*www.chillibird.com.au*

**CCN – Cross Country Nurseries/ChilePlants.com (USA)**
*www.chileplants.com*

**CF – The Chilli Factory (Australia)**
*www.thechillifactory.com*

**CH – Chillihead.co.za (South Africa)**
*www.chillihead.co.za*

**CSB – Chilli Seed Bank (Australia)**
*www.chilliseedbank.com.au*

**CSU – Chile Seed USA (USA)**
*www.chileseedusa.com*

**CT – Chili Taarn (Denmark)**
*www.chilitarn.dk*

**FS – Fatalii Seeds (Finland)**
*www.fataliiseeds.net*

**HS – The Hippy Seed Company (Australia)**
*www.thehippyseedcompany.com*

**LS – Livingseeds (South Africa)**
*www.livingseeds.co.za*

**MWCH – Midwest Chileheads LLC (USA)**
*www.midwestchileheads.com*

**NMSU – NMSU Chile Pepper Institute (USA)**
*www.chilepepperinstitute.org*

**NN – Nicky's Nursery Ltd (UK)**
*www.nickys-nursery.co.uk*

**PBPC – PuckerButt Pepper Company (USA)**
*www.puckerbuttpeppercompany.com*

**PJ – Pepper Joe's (USA)**
*www.pepperjoe.com*

**PN – Pepper North (Canada)**
*www.peppernorth.com*

**PSEU – Pepperseeds.eu (Netherlands)**
*www.pepperseeds.eu*

**PZW– Peperzadenwinkel.be (Belgium)**
*www.peperzadenwinkel.be*

**RFC – Refining Fire Chiles (USA)**
*www.superhotchiles.com*

**RMR – Reimer Seeds (USA)**
*www.reimerseeds.com*

**SDCF – South Devon Chilli Farm (UK)**
*www.southdevonchillifarm.co.uk*

**SLP – Semillas La Palma (Spain)**
*www.semillas.de*

**SS – Simpson's Seeds (UK)**
*www.simpsonsseeds.co.uk*

**SSS – Sea Spring Seeds (UK)**
*www.seaspringseeds.co.uk*

**TCPC – The Chilli Pepper Company (UK)**
*www.thechillipeppercompany.co.uk*

**TF – Tyler Farms (USA)**
*www.tyler-farms.com*

**TWF – Trade Winds Fruit (USA)**
*www.tradewindsfruit.com*

**UKCS – UK Chilli Seeds (UK)**
*www.ukchilliseeds.co.uk*

**VNG – Victoriana Nursery Gardens (UK)**
*www.victoriananursery.co.uk*

# Acknowledgements

## Author acknowledgements

Thanks to all the chilli enthusiasts that put up with my calls, emails and visits over the six months it has taken to collect and verify the information I needed to write this book. Special thanks goes to Joy Michaud at Sea Spring Seeds and Matt Simpson of Simpson Seeds who lucky for me are based just a few miles from me.

I must also thanks my family who have had to put up with so many visit to chilli farms and events over the past decades. So thanks to wife Sonia and the kids, Nick, Jason, Lizzi, Antony and Mary. Another special thanks to Edna my mother without whom there would be a lot more mistakes in the text.

## Picture credits

**123RF** bruno135 2. **Alamy** 67photo 205; Adrian Sherratt 202, 212, 216; Antony Nettle 208; Antony Ratcliffe 182; Banos 39; Clare Gainey 53, 121; franco pizzochero/MARKA 78; Jamie Pham Photography 111; John Glover 57; Keith Mayhew 47; Malcolm Park food images 44; Mim Friday 131; Nikreates 42, 148; OnWhite 176; Rex May 101, 113, 155; Richard Ellis 73; Ryan B. Stevenson 32; Teubner Foodfoto/Bon Appetit 94. **Buckeye Pepper Company** 81, 159, 171. **ChilePlants.com** 69, 83, 85, 99, 107, 139, 185, 187, 19, 23, 67. **chilitaarn.dk** 173. **Chilli Pepper Institute New Mexico State University** 76. **Christopher Phillips** 145, 169. **Dreamstime.com** Anphotos 60; Bert Folsom 20; Bhofack2 63; Daniel Novoa 116; Lucie Lang 180; Lunamarina 88; Mrsixinthemix 220; Msheldrake 48; Ngoc Thu Nguyen Ho 166; Pamela Panella 178, 200; Paulpaladin 96; Pipa100 40, 126; Ppy2010ha 92; Ryan Stevenson 90; Tgshutter 36; Thomas Dutour 65; Vinicius Tupinamba 28; Zigzagmtart 54. **Enrico Lai AKA "The Mojo Pepper"** (mojopepper.blogspot.com) 190; **fataliiseeds.net** Jukka Kilpinen 214. **GAP Photos** Heather Edwards 51, 157; Juliette Wade 151; Lynn Keddie 198; Nicola Stocken 31. **Garden World Images** Lee Thomas 119; William Clevitt 133. **Hans-Joachim Baader, www.hjbaader.de** 109. **iStock** Dvdovalina 143; YinYang 74. **Matt Simpson/www.simpsonseeds.co.uk** 27. **Phil Gremillion, Farms of Papa Jeabert, USA** 105. **picturesofus.net** Desmond Johnson 123. **Rep07** 129. **Sea Spring Seeds** 25, 34, 103, 137, 141, 153, 161, 17. **Shutterstock** bonchan 14, swa182 189. **The Garden Collection** FP/Martin Hughes-Jones 13. **The Hippy Seed Company** 195. **Thinkstock** fotoduki 174. **Toms Treibhaus** Thomas Schneider 125. **Tuttodipeperoncini.com** Giancarlo 115. **ukchilliseeds.co.uk** 70, 146, 164, 197, 206, 218. **Victoriana Nursery Gardens** 87. **www.sowchillies.co.uk** 135.